W9-ATE-504

Table of Contents

Note to the Teacher

Finally, a biblically-centered world history course for young children! And along with that, **it's fun**. This light-hearted approach to history makes a wonderful first impression on young children, allowing them to discover that learning is enjoyable: talking about people, solving word puzzles, making crafts, singing songs . . . all with the purpose of learning what God has done in history.

Our curriculum utilizes the latest information on how people learn best. Woven into its presentational fabric are the visual, auditory, and kinesthetic learning modalities and the four learning styles of Feeler, Thinker, Sensor, Intuitor (Meyers-Briggs system). You don't have to hold a PhD in educational psychology (or know anything about these various learning grids) to be able to use our curriculum— whether you do or not, you can rest assured that there will be a connection that appeals to each of your unique learners.

Feeler: A "People" Person

- wants to know the subjective, people perspective

Thinker: A "Facts" Person

- wants to know the objective, factual perspective

Sensor: A "Hands-On" Person

- wants to learn through hands-on, sensory experiences

Intuitor: An "Idea" Person

- wants to be involved in creative expressions

This *Elementary Activity Book* uses four phases per chapter, which correspond to the four learning styles mentioned above. Do not be concerned if you are unable to recognize the particular learning style of your student—this four-phase approach gives a wide variety of experiences, greatly enhancing each student's grasp of history in every time period. If you are simultaneously teaching older students using the *Romans, Reformers, Revolutionaries* curriculum, you will be able to easily and simply coordinate activities your younger students are doing with those of older students in each of the four phases.

Phase One is the **Introduction Time**, corresponding to the **Feeler** Learning Style. In this phase you will:

- read Bible stories and articles about important people
- share discussion questions
- discover "Fascinating Folks" & "Exciting Events"
- find suggestions for other books to read

Note: In the reading and discussion, create a comfortable atmosphere where your students can ask questions and explore ideas with freedom. Spread out the stories, one or two per day, unless your children are clamoring for more.

Phase Two is the **Exploration & Discovery Time**, corresponding to the **Thinker** Learning Style. In this phase, you will be playing with vocabulary words in:

- Scrambles
- Word searches
- Crossword puzzles

Note: Sit side by side with your students to do the vocabulary puzzles. Even if they don't know how to read, if they recognize some letters, you can solve the various puzzles. Chat together about the meanings of the vocabulary words until your children are comfortable with them.

Phase Three is the **Hands-On Time**, corresponding to the **Sensor** Learning Style. In this phase, you will:

- experiment with simple science projects
- create child-friendly crafts
- fix (and eat!) "Fun Food"
- color the maps or find your way through the mazes.

Note: Take your time with these hands-on projects. We suggest that you only do one per day so your students have plenty of opportunity to enjoy the experience.

Phase Four is the **Expression Time**, corresponding to the **Intuitor** Learning Style. In this phase you may:

- create your own masterpiece
- perform in an "Acting-Up History" skit
- sing a "Somewhat Silly Song"
- rollick in "Rhyme Time"
- move in an "Action Activity"
- play a "Goofy Game"

Note: If you're doing "Acting-Up History," it could take an entire week to learn lines, make costumes, find props, and collect an audience. Some of the other expression activities could be accomplished in one session. The main point is to let the learning experience be enjoyable.

FAQs

Q. How long should we spend on each phase?

A. If you spend one week per phase, you would then complete each unit in one month, and the entire book would be finished in nine months. However, please feel free to take a longer or a shorter amount of time if that works better for your students.

Q. How long should we spend each day?

A. Young children should not spend hours per day on academic work, as they are not yet physically, mentally, or emotionally ready! Instead of coercing your impressionable learners into a formalized, regimented approach to education, our curriculum easily accommodates their own natural way of receiving information: we will be reading out loud, talking together, coloring pictures, making crafts, doing science experiments, playing games, singing songs, reading, and coloring maps. You could realistically spend thirty minutes, two or three times a week, and complete all the projects. However, if students are enjoying what they are doing and would like to continue "playing" with history, feel free to follow their personal timetable. They will learn and retain far more, and with more enthusiasm, than can be expected from the rigidity of a traditional curriculum.

Q. How do I test my children to see if they have learned enough?

A. Test them by listening to them: listen to their answers, listen to their conversations with others, listen to their questions. The discussion questions listed are to give you a start at dialoguing with your children. As both of you learn to share the wonder, it will be a growing experience!

Q. How will I know if they miss anything?

A. History is everything that has happened since the moment of creation until the present. It is simply too large a subject to expect that children (or adults) will know everything about it. However, I guarantee that few elementary age children will know as much about the middle ages and church history as your children, once they complete this course!

AUDIO RECORDINGS!

Much of the foundational teaching for this book, as well as for the *Romans, Reformers, Revolutionaries* curriculum, is found in the four-disc audio series *What in the World?—Volume Two*. We suggest that you use this audio presentation to gain an overview in your study of the Middle Ages and Church history. The recordings are interesting, exciting, and fun to listen to—even for students in the early elementary grades!

The Rise of the Church
& the Fall of Rome

Pentecost

Bible History to Read and Talk About

Ascension of Jesus: Acts 1:1–11

- Why did Jesus want his disciples to stay in Jerusalem for a time? Do you think Peter and the other disciples needed to receive God's power in their lives? Why or why not?

- Where did Jesus tell his disciples that they would go to be witnesses? Was it far from their homes? Why do you think Jesus would want his friends to go to faraway places? Would it be hard to do that? Why or why not?

- Do you think the disciples were sad or unhappy or scared when Jesus went to heaven? Why or why not? What did the two men in white clothes say to the disciples when Jesus went up into heaven? Why would it be helpful to the disciples to have Jesus's promise that He was coming back? How is it helpful to us today to have this same promise?

Day of Pentecost: Acts 2:1–41

- What happened on the day of Pentecost? Do you think the people in the upper room were surprised? Astonished? Scared? Happy? Excited?

- There had been Jews from all over the world in Jerusalem on the day of Pentecost. Name the countries the people were from. What did they say and do when the Holy Spirit came to Jesus's disciples? Do you think they were surprised? Astonished? Scared? Happy? Excited?

- What did Peter do when some people said

that the disciples were drunk? Do you think Peter was acting differently than he had when Jesus was taken to be crucified? Why or why not? If your answer is "Yes," what made the difference? What was the result of Peter's preaching?

Conversion of Saul: Acts 8:1–4, 9:1–22

What did Saul do to people who believed in Jesus? Do you think Saul was a scary man to the followers of Jesus? Why or why not?

What happened to Saul when he was going to Damascus? Why was it hard for Ananias to go see Saul? What would you have done if you had been in Ananias' shoes?

After Saul's conversion, what were some of the things he did? What response did he receive from the Jews? From the Hellenists (Greeks)? Where did the believers send him? What was the result? How did that help solve the problems the Christians were having?

Saul, whose name was changed to Paul, went on to become a messenger of God's good news to the world beyond Israel. His many missionary journeys took him from the Middle East, throughout the Mediterranean, and all the way to Europe. Just as Jesus had told his disciples, they became witnesses of Him in Jerusalem, Judea, Samaria, and they even began going unto the uttermost parts of the earth. Read more about it in the Book of Acts!

Fascinating Folks & Exciting Events

Nero and the Burning of Rome (AD 64)

Roman emperors were very powerful people. Because the army, who had the force to accomplish imperial commands, was totally loyal to the Emperor, there was no one who could stop a bad emperor from doing evil and horrible things. One of the worst was the Emperor Nero. He was so afraid that someone in his family would try to take over and become emperor in his place that he even killed his step-brother and his mother! Then he began to kill anyone who angered him.

Everyone in Rome feared and distrusted Emperor Nero—with good reason! When a devastating fire broke out in Rome, Nero decided to rebuild the city. However, his greatest efforts were in building himself a huge and magnificent new palace. People whispered among themselves that Nero had set the fire on purpose so he could watch it burn and then claim the land for himself. When he heard that the people were against him, he said he was innocent and would never do that. He said it was the Christians who started the fire! He used this story as an excuse to kill many Christian believers, including Peter and Paul. Eventually, the people of Rome had had enough of Nero, and he ended up being killed by a servant.

Constantine's Conversion (AD 312)

At this point in history, two incredible events occurred in the Roman Empire. The first was when a young man with a small army convinced an emperor with a large army to fight a battle outside of the protection of the walls of Rome - and he WON! The young man was Constantine, and his winning the battle of Milvian Bridge was considered almost a miracle by the people of Rome. The second incredible event was when Constantine announced to the Empire that Christians were no longer to be persecuted, and

that, in fact, he himself was a Christian! This had a dramatic effect upon the Christian Church. Because the Emperor himself proclaimed Christianity to be good, a huge number of people joined the Church—probably to gain favor with the Emperor rather than because of a true conversion experience. This meant that, though the persecution of Christians was a thing of the past, now the Church was being filled up with people who were bringing their pagan beliefs with them.

Athanasius and the Council of Nicea (AD 325)

With Christianity now the favored religion in the Empire, many strange ideas about Jesus came forth from various teachers. One man, Arius, was especially good at teaching these strange ideas since he could write catchy songs to help people learn the new beliefs. Arius taught that Jesus was not really God but more like a superhero created by God. Many people supported this Arian doctrine because it was similar to the idea of the Greek gods and goddesses, which were more familiar to them.

However, one leader in the Church fought like a lion to stop the spread of this new idea. His name was Athanasius. He believed what the Scriptures taught: that Jesus was fully God, of the same substance as God, that Jesus was with God from the beginning, and was not a part of the created world. When Emperor Constantine called together the leaders of the Church at the Council of Nicea to end the arguing about Arius's teaching, Athanasius forcefully presented this true perspective from Scripture. The people at the council were convinced that his position was the correct one, and they decided that Arius's teachings were heresy (false). You can read what the Council of Nicea decided was true Christian belief by reading the Nicene Creed. It can be found in hymnals, or ask your pastor.

Word Search

Using the words from your vocabulary list at the bottom of the page, search for words in the puzzle. The words are diagonal, vertical, and horizontal. Have fun!

```
W A E D I U W B S A C O N S A T I E P
B L X R A M A N T I O C H E R I M B A
I M N C A T N C R D C U E G I O S T U
D C A R O M E S L K H R L D F B N A L
J O T P Y N A M N A E X R E M N E G F
A S C H A S S F O T R M M O G F S A W
L N H P U G L T U D M Y C M A I G C A
E G U H C S Y C A R I A H H T P O K L
X I R I H A E H J N T I I A U P L N E
A S T P J S H U S A T H T N D R Y E X
N A Y T R E W I C I H I K T Y R C R K
D C L E E P A L P S U P N T M A I H A
R K P M S O M I W P S Q R E E C R A M
I C P O L Y C A R P O A O T L Y P D N
A T R I E A N P Y O M R M R O O T R R
K E O H G K P T G E V T N A T L E A I
N Q P G W Y C O N V E R T H P P L I A
```

Alexandria	Antioch	catacombs	Church	Constantine
convert	Hadrian	hermit	Hippo	hymn
icthus	legion	martyr	Nero	Paul
persecute	Polycarp	Ptolemy	Rome	sack

Hands-On History Fun
Create-A-Craft:

Catacomb Art on the Sidewalk

Early in the history of the Church, the Christians in Rome often met for services in the catacombs, which are underground burial sites. Some of the Christians were wonderful artists who painted pictures about events from the Bible on the walls of the catacombs. Why not share with your family and neighbors about Bible events by doing "catacomb style" sidewalk art?

You will need: Large, colored chalk; ½ cup sugar; 1½ cups water; sidewalk or butcher paper

Combine the sugar and water, stir to mix. Soak the chalk in the sugar solution for 3–4 minutes. Then, draw pictures from the Bible, such as Noah's Ark, creation of the sun and moon, the cross of Jesus, the empty tomb, etc. Soak your chalk again when it dries out.

Fun Foods to Fix:

Painted "Fish" Toast

Try your hand at making an ICTHUS, the Christian symbol of a fish that the early Christians used to identify one another. (In Greek, it is spelled "ΙΧΘΥΣ.") Though they would make their drawing in the sand, you can make it on toast—and then eat it!

You will need: ½ cup milk, divided into 2 containers; green food coloring; blue food coloring; new paint brush or clean pastry brush; 1 slice of bread per person; butter and sugar for spreading on toast

Place several drops of food coloring into the milk (one container of milk per color). Using either a new paint brush or clean pastry brush, paint a fish on the bread. Toast the bread and observe your fish symbol. Would your Christian friend recognize it? Lightly spread with butter and sugar if you wish. Remember, this is "icthus," not icky!

Marvelous Mazes!

Join with Paul as he travels the path from his encounter with God along the Damascus Road all the way to Rome.

Damascus Road

Along the way, you will visit the cities of Lystra and Derbe, where the people hated Paul so much for preaching the gospel of Jesus Christ that they stoned him; you will spend a night in Troas, where Paul had a vision of a man from Macedonia pleading with him to come there; you will listen as Paul delivers a speech to the philosophers and worshipers on Mars Hill in Athens, Greece; and you will dive off the sinking ship with him and swim to shore on the island of Malta.

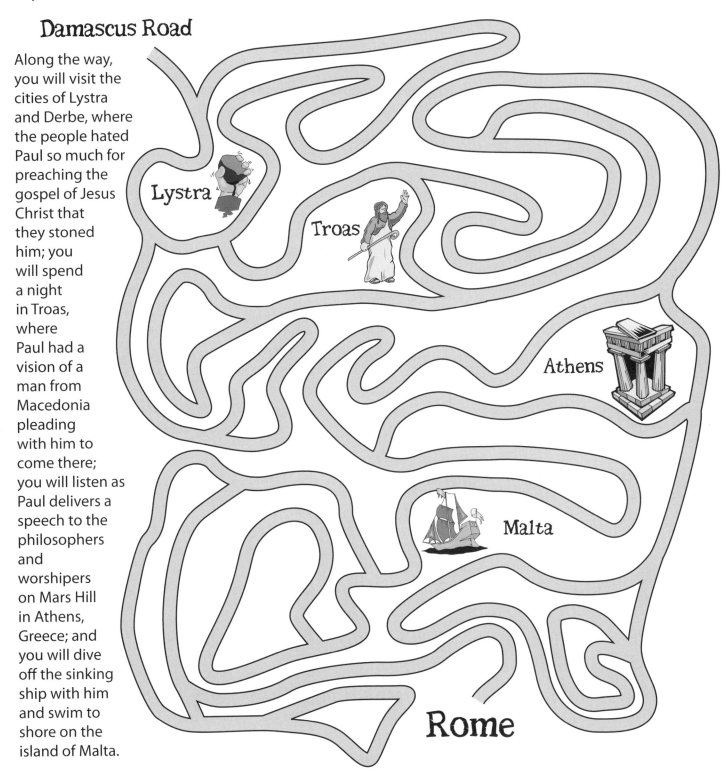

Lystra

Troas

Athens

Malta

Rome

Your Own Masterpiece

Draw a picture depicting a story from the book of Acts.

Creative Fun with History!
Going Goofy Game:

Gospel Explosion

This game is to demonstrate that safe Roman roads and the common Greek language allowed the Gospel to explode throughout the world in the first few centuries after Jesus's ascension.

Six or more players needed (if you have fewer than six people, "Roman Road" and "Greek Language" may be played by the same person):

> **"Christian," who proclaims in a loud voice, "I have Good News!"**
>
> **"Roman Road, " who frequently proclaims, "Safe roads,"**
>
> **"Greek Language," who frequently proclaims, "Get it?"**
>
> **"Jew" (may be played by more than one player)**
>
> **"Samaritan" (may be played by more than one player)**
>
> **"Far-Away-Foreigner" (may be played by more than one player)**

In a large area, preferably outside, set up a course of orbits around a center point. Mark the center point using a brightly colored cloth, or paper plate, etc., and call that place "Jerusalem." In a similar way, mark another spot ten or more feet away to indicate the first orbit—call it "Judea"—and a third spot ten or more feet away to show the second orbit, "Samaria." Finally, mark a spot ten feet beyond that for the outside orbit and call it "The Uttermost Parts." The children will be running around these orbits similar to the orbits of planets. If they have a hard time visualizing their course, place more markers around each orbit for them to follow.

Gather the players into a tight circle at Jerusalem. Have the smallest player be "Christian," the largest players be "Roman Road" and "Greek Language." Have everyone count together out loud, "One, Two, Three, GO!"

At this point, the player (players) called "Jew" starts running around outside of the group in a circuit that follows your first orbit, in Judea. As soon as all "Jews" are out and have run a complete circuit, the player (players) called "Samaritan" needs to run out to the second orbit and run in a circle around the center at that marker (similar to the orbits of the planets).

As soon as all "Samaritans" make a complete circuit, the player (players) called "Far-Away-Foreigner" needs to run to the outside marked spot and run a circuit around the "uttermost parts." Or, all the players could leave Jerusalem at once!

"Roman Road" and "Greek Language" carry "Christian" (or if this is too difficult, they may take "Christian" by the hand), run out as a unit around the orbits, all proclaiming loudly, and tag the other players as they run around their orbits. They need to first tag all players representing "Jew," next "Samaritan," then "Far-Away-Foreigner."

When one is tagged, he must freeze and say three times in a loud voice, "I have received the Good News!" After this, the tagged one joins with "Christian's" group and helps to tag the remaining players.

Missionaries
& Barbarians

Patrick, missionary to Ireland

Bible Verses to Read & Talk About

The Great Commission: Matthew 28:18–20; Mark 16:15–16

- Where did Jesus tell his disciples to go? What did he tell them to do?

- Talk together about becoming a missionary ("sent one"). What kinds of adventures and difficulties do missionaries have? Why do missionaries go to faraway places? What kind of preparation would be good for missionaries to have before they go?

We heartily recommend reading missionary biographies to your children. One of the best series around is *Christian Heroes: Then & Now* by Janet & Geoff Benge, available from your local book supplier, or from YWAM Publishing (800) 922-2143.

Preaching the Gospel: Romans 10:13–15

- Consider together: how do people learn about Jesus? Name the questions that are asked in this Scripture passage. How would you answer those questions?

- Why do you think the Bible says that the feet of those who preach the gospel are beautiful? What makes them beautiful? Who thinks they are beautiful? (Hint: Consider the people in the world who have never before heard about Jesus.)

Ambassadors for Christ: 2 Corinthians 5:17–21

- Talk together about what it means to be a new creation in Christ. Is that good news? Why or why not? What effect might there be in someone's life when they become a new creation? Consider this when you learn in this chapter about the barbarians who were converted to Christianity.

- What is an ambassador? Who does an ambassador represent? Where does an ambassador work? Talk about what it means to be an ambassador of Christ. What is our message? What does it mean to be reconciled?

Suggested Books for Reading Together

***Famous Men of the Middle Ages* by John H. Haaren & A. B. Poland**

Short, interesting biographies of fascinating personalities from the Middle Ages, this book is a wonderful introduction for all ages. It includes such people as Justinian (Byzantine), Mohammed (Islam), Charlemagne, Francis of Assisi, Marco Polo, and Gutenberg. Several biographies of barbarian leaders are included. Highly recommended!

***Barbarians, Christians, and Muslims—The Cambridge Introduction to History* by Trevor Cairns**

Fascinating, well-written account of the barbarian tribes, the Byzantine empire, and the growth of Islam. This book has lots of pictures and maps, and if adults read it to their younger students, it is a wonderful introduction to the topic!

Fascinating Folks & Exciting Events

Patrick Goes to Ireland (c. 390–461)

Patrick was born in Britain, which was at that time ruled by the Romans. When barbarians began invading Rome, the Roman army left Britain to defend its own homeland. This made an opening for fierce Irish slave traders to come to the defenseless British shores, capture people and take them back to Ireland. Patrick was captured in this way when he was sixteen years old and taken as a slave to Ireland. Though he knew the Gospel before his capture, becoming a slave made him earnest toward God! After six long years, Patrick managed to escape from his master and flee Ireland in a trading boat. When he returned home, his parents were ecstatic since they had long before given him up for dead. Imagine their surprise and dismay when he told them about his dream that little Irish children were calling out asking him to come back to them! He eventually returned to Ireland and began preaching and teaching the Good News about Jesus Christ. In his nearly thirty years of missionary work in Ireland, almost the entire island was converted to Christianity—without a single martyr.

Columba Evangelizes Scotland (521–597)

Born as a part of the nobility of Ireland, Columba was destined by his parents for the priesthood. As a young boy, he lived as a foster son with a priest so that he could be trained to be a priest. Eventually, when he became a man, he was made a leader in the church. But, because he was the cause of a massive battle concerning who owned a portion of Scripture, he was sent away forever from his home in Ireland so that he might win the souls of as many men as were lost in that battle. That is what many of the stories of Columba say, but no one is really sure of Columba's reasons for sailing to Iona, the island off the coast of Scotland. He founded a monastery there from which many, many monks went out to preach the gospel around the world, including Brendan the Navigator—who may have actually sailed all the way to North America! There are many stories of the miracles Columba did in Scotland and of the incredible influence he had on the people. Through his ministry, Christianity became a vital aspect of this area that had been previously considered impossibly barbaric and heathen. It is interesting to compare Columba with Patrick who went to Ireland from Christian England . . . Then, Columba went to Scotland from Christian Ireland . . . Then, Scottish and Irish monks went back into England to bring the Gospel to the new barbarian rulers!!!

Attila the Hun, the Scourge of God (ruled 433–453)

It is funny how people can view one man from such different perspectives. For instance, Attila the Hun was called "Scourge of God" by the Western Europeans, "Father of Hungary" by the Hungarians, and a "great leader" by the Germans! As a boy, Attila was sent to Rome to be a hostage since he was the king's son. This was a sort of promise to the Romans that his tribe would be on their best behavior! However, during his time there, Attila saw how corrupt the Roman people were. He made a vow that he would always live a simple, "Spartan" life so that he might defeat the Roman Empire. When he returned home, Attila became a powerful military leader of the Huns. They made war on the Romans whenever possible, and usually won! The people in Western Europe trembled when they heard Attila's name since he was such a dangerous man. However, the people who followed him considered Attila a great and powerful ruler. The people of Hungary consider themselves to be the heirs of Attila's empire. That's why they call him the "Father of Hungary!"

Crossword Puzzle

Using the clues below and the words from your vocabulary list, fill in the crossword puzzle.

army
attack
Attila
barbarian
boats
Boniface
captive
Celtic
civilize
Columba
converts
defend
Hun
illumine
invade
journeys
missionary
monastery
navigate
Patrick
resist
slaves
tribe
voyage

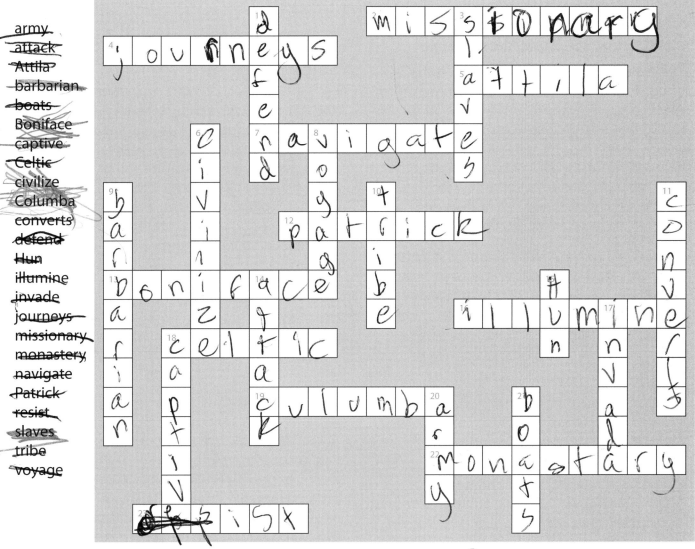

Across

2. Columba was a _____ to Scotland.
4. Brendan the Navigator made many _____.
5. The leader of the Huns.
7. To sail or steer a ship.
12. He brought the gospel to Ireland.
13. Early missionary to Germany.
16. When the monks would decorate the Scriptures.
18. Pertaining to the culture of the British Isles.
19. The Irish monk who became a missionary to Scotland.
22. Where monks live and work together.
23. To oppose.

Down

1. To guard from attack.
3. People owned by other people
6. To change from a primitive way of life.
8. Journey by water.
9. A member of an uncivilized people.
10. A group of people sharing the same customs, language, and ancestors.
11. People who changed their beliefs because of missionaries.
14. To begin fighting against.
15. Attila the _____.
17. To enter with force as an enemy.
18. A person captured and held unwillingly.
20. An organized group of soldiers trained and armed for war.
21. Small open vessels for traveling on water.

Hands-On History Fun
Create-A-Craft:

Illustrate the Scriptures, Collage Style

This exercise will help your younger students understand a little bit about the lovely art form that was used by monks to "illumine" or illustrate the Scriptures they were copying by hand. These illuminated scriptures were very precise and demanding, but, in order to keep young artists from being frustrated with their handiwork, we recommend trying this simpler creation of a collage to illustrate a portion of Scripture.

You will need: A short piece of Scripture, printed on white paper (perhaps Matthew 28:18–20); Several colorful magazines suitable for cutting with scissors; Construction paper of various colors;

Marking pens and/or crayons; Glue; Scissors

From the magazines, help your student choose and remove several pictures that illustrate or explain the Scripture passage. If you would prefer, your students may draw their own pictures around the Scripture you write out on clean white paper. Arrange them around the perimeter of the words in a way that pleases your eye. Cut out several large shapes from construction paper of various colors to arrange around and behind the magazine pictures. When it looks the way you want it to, carefully glue each piece to the white paper. You might want to finish this illustrated Scripture with marking pens or crayons.

Fun Food to Fix:

Make Missionary Boats, Complete with Monks

You will need: 2 ounces of soft-style cream cheese (you may substitute peanut butter if you prefer); 2 celery stalks, cut into two-inch lengths to create "boats"; 2 tablespoons raisins; One toothpick per each two-inch celery "boat"; One paper triangle per each celery "boat"; Masking tape

Spread each celery stalk "boat" with either cream cheese or peanut butter. Set several raisins upright in the boat to represent the Irish monks who sailed the seas to spread the Gospel. Tape each paper triangle to a toothpick, and firmly affix your sail to the "boat"! You may want to sail your celery boats to various plates on the table. Perhaps, if you want to be Brendan the Navigator, you will be sailing as far as North America. Be sure to remove the toothpicks and sails before eating your boats!

Where in the World . . .
is Ireland?

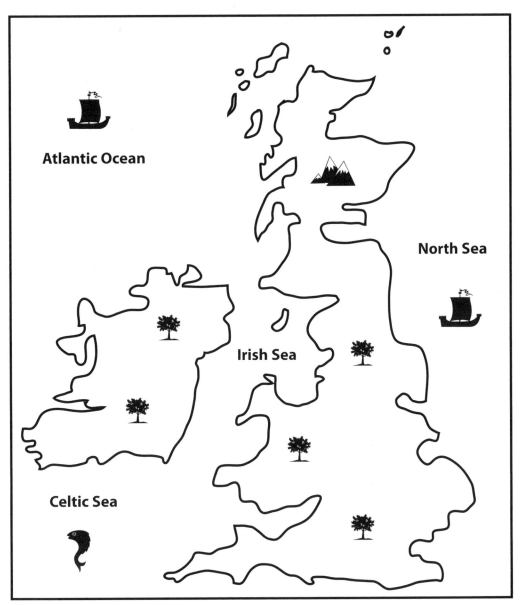

Color the areas around these:

 purple mountains green vegetation blue water

Clues for finding Ireland:

- I am WEST of the Irish Sea.
- I am NORTH of the Celtic Sea.
- I am in the Atlantic Ocean.

Where am I?

Your Own Masterpiece

Draw a picture depicting Patrick chasing the snakes out of Ireland.

Creative Fun with History!

Singing Somewhat Silly Songs:

Attila, O-Attil-ee-o the Hun (to the tune of "Polly Wally Doodle")

Oh, he came from a tribe, a tribe of Huns,
Sing Attila, O-Attil-ee-o the Hun
By the time he finished, his work was done.
Sing Attila, O-Attil-ee-o the Hun

Chorus:
Here he comes, here he comes,
Here he comes to conquer Rome.
For he saw that they were weakened,
And he knew that he could take 'em.
Sing Attila, O-Attil-ee-o the Hun

Well, he went to Rome as a hostage lad,
Sing Attila, O-Attil-ee-o the Hun
He looked around, saw Rome was bad.
Sing Attila, O-Attil-ee-o the Hun

Ae-ti-us was his Roman friend,
Sing Attila, O-Attil-ee-o the Hun
His friend was General in the end.
Sing Attila, O-Attil-ee-o the Hun

Chorus

He met this friend at battle time,
Sing Attila, O-Attil-ee-o the Hun
But they were on opposing sides.
Sing Attila, O-Attil-ee-o the Hun

Attila lost to Ae-ti-us that day,
Sing Attila, O-Attil-ee-o the Hun
But he vowed he'd take Rome anyway.
Sing Attila, O-Attil-ee-o the Hun

Chorus

When next he came to conquer Rome,
Sing Attila, O-Attil-ee-o the Hun
Pope Leo begged him to go home.
Sing Attila, O-Attil-ee-o the Hun

And then one fateful day he wed,
Sing Attila, O-Attil-ee-o the Hun
And died of a nosebleed in his head.
Sing Attila, O-Attil-ee-o the Hun

UNIT 3
Byzantines & Muslims

Justinian the Great

Bible Verses to Read & Talk About

The Deity of the Messiah: Isaiah 9:6–7; Luke 2:8–14

Who is Jesus? The Koran (Islam's holy book) teaches about Jesus, but He is considered to be only a prophet. Muslims believe that Mohammed was the final prophet, and that he gave the final and fullest understanding of the One God. Read these Scriptures together and talk about the Bible's description of who Jesus is.

- How does the scripture in Isaiah describe the Messiah? What are some of the names given?

- Why did the angels appear to the shepherds? How did they describe the one who was born that day in the city of David?

- What do you think these scriptures teach us about Jesus' nature? Is He God? Is He man? Is He both?

God the Father: Matthew 3:16–17; John 10:27–30, 17:20–21

- What do these Scriptures show us about Jesus's relationship to God? Is this a special, unique relationship? Why or why not?

The Father Heart of God: Romans 8:14–15; 2 Corinthians 6:18; 1 John 3:1

A Muslim believes that Allah (the One God) is all-knowing, all-powerful, creator, and sovereign over all. They often say, "If Allah wills" in response to troubling situations. However, there is no understanding of the intimate, Father-to-child personal relationship, which the Bible describes as the privilege of the believer. Read these Scriptures together and talk about what God offers to us.

- How does the Bible describe the relationship we may have with God? What do you think it would be like to be a Christian if God did NOT adopt us as His children?

Jesus's Sacrificial Death: John 3:16, 10:11–18

Though Islam teaches that Allah is holy and will judge each person according to his or her deeds, there is no such thing as forgiveness of sins or a Savior who loved us enough to die in order to bring us redemption. Read these Scriptures together to see the Bible's message about what Jesus came to accomplish and WHY He did it.

- Jesus described his coming death in this second passage of Scripture. For whom did Jesus say He was laying down His life? Do you think Jesus was surprised when He was taken to be crucified? Why or why not?

- Talk together about the purpose of Jesus's death on the cross. Why did Jesus come to die?

What should be our response to this?

Suggested Books for Reading Together

Barbarians, Christians, and Muslims—The Cambridge Introduction to History by Trevor Cairns

Fascinating, well-written account of the barbarian tribes, the Byzantine empire, and the growth of Islam. This book has lots of pictures and maps, and, if adults read it to their younger students, it is a wonderful introduction to the topic!

The Arabs in the Golden Age by Mokhtar Moktefi & Veronique Ageorges

Very colorful, well-written book about the Muslim Empire.

Fascinating Folks & Exciting Events

The Reign of Justinian the Great (527–565)

Though the western part of the Roman Empire had fallen to barbarian conquerors in the 400s, the eastern part (known as the Byzantine Empire) still had an emperor, an imperial city (Constantinople), and a powerful army. When Justinian became the Byzantine emperor in 527, he determined to regain areas of the Roman Empire that had been taken by the barbarians. His powerful army reconquered North Africa from the Vandals and took back Italy (including Rome) from the Ostrogoths. This was an amazing accomplishment but very expensive! Justinian built beautiful buildings for the city of Constantinople, including Hagia Sophia, one of the most incredible churches ever built! This was also an amazing accomplishment, but, again, very expensive. Justinian's greatest effort, however, was simplifying the old Roman laws (which contained over three million lines of writing!) to the Code of Laws (which contained only one hundred-fifty thousand lines of writing). This made the law very understandable and usable for everyone in the Empire. When Justinian died, the Byzantine Empire had good laws, beautiful churches, more territory . . . but it was all very expensive. What a tremendous debt! This debt weakened the empire and made it vulnerable to attack.

Mohammed and the birth of Islam (c. 570–632)

Arabia is a land of desert, steppe, and an occasional oasis. The people who lived there made their living mostly by working on caravans or herding their flocks of animals from one oasis to the next. In 570, a boy named Mohammed was born here and became a camel driver on the caravans. Perhaps it was those caravan trips to other parts of the Middle East that allowed him to learn about Judaism and Christianity.

Most of the Arabs of this time believed in many gods, and they came to a city called Mecca in order to offer animal sacrifices to these gods. However, he rejected all these religions and told people that he had visions of the angel Gabriel teaching him that there was only one God, and his name is Allah. This was a serious threat to the city of Mecca, the place where many gods were worshipped, and people reacted violently to his new idea. So, in the year 622, Mohammed fled across the desert to a city called Medina where he was received as the Prophet of Allah. This flight to Medina is known as the Hegira and is the year the Muslims date as Year One in their calendar. Eventually, Mohammed raised an army of believers in Medina who marched with him to conquer Mecca. They were so powerful that the people of Mecca surrendered without a fight.

By the time of Mohammed's death in 632, most of the Arabs had become Muslims. In the next 100 years, Islam (the religion of the Muslims) swept the Middle East, North Africa (part of the Byzantine Empire), the Persian Empire, and Spain through the military might of the newly-inspired Arabs. Europe gave a huge sigh of relief when the Muslim advance was stopped in France at the Battle of Tours in 732.

Word Scrambles

Unscramble the words to spell out people, places, or things that have to do with your study of Byzantines and Muslims. Look at the vocabulary list below for possible answers, and don't get too "mixed Up!"

doxortoh _____

yzantineb _____

squemo _____

slimmu _____

lahal _____

arba _____

quescont _____

coni _____

caphil _____

kgree rife _____

graphcalyil _____

trtionadi _____

jidha _____

icamos _____

mode _____

jutinisan _____

mmedhamo _____

camec _____

gedlon hrno _____

stannopleconti _____

Allah	Arab	Byzantine	Caliph	Calligraphy
Conquest	Constantinople	Dome	Greek Fire	Golden horn
Icon	Jihad	Justinian	Mecca	Mosaic
Muslim	Mohammed	Mosque	Orthodox	Tradition

Hands-On History Fun
Create-A-Craft:

Dyed Cotton Bracelets

When the Arabs conquered other countries in the name of Allah, they learned many wonderful scientific, mathematical, and agricultural ideas from the conquered people. The Muslim Arabs built on this foundation of knowledge and introduced many new products and ideas to the rest of the world. It was the Arab civilization that developed agricultural techniques for growing cotton, and also they who presented cotton fabric to the rest of the world!

You will need: 3 cotton balls per student (real cotton, not synthetic); 3 packages of unsweetened drink mix of different colors ("Kool-Aid") (blue, green, and red are nice for this project); Boiling water; Bowls; Paper towels

CAUTION: ADULT SUPERVISION REQUIRED. Carefully pull each cotton ball until it unwinds into about a 2–3" length. Don't worry if it breaks apart, it can be reattached after dying. Place ½ teaspoon of unsweetened drink mix in a bowl. Add ½ cup boiling water to the drink mix and stir gently until powder dissolves. Put one cotton length for each student into the bowl. Repeat for the other two colors. Let the cotton sit in the dye for five minutes. Then remove from the bowl with a fork (allowing the liquid to drip off the cotton and into the bowl) and place upon several folded paper towels. MAKE SURE THE DIFFERENT COLORS DO NOT TOUCH OR THEY WILL BLEED. Let dry overnight in a warm place.

When the cotton lengths are dried, give one of each color to each student. The students need to carefully twist each length of cotton (a simple form of spinning) in order to strengthen it. If there are pieces of cotton that have pulled apart, help the student reattach them by twisting the cotton piece on to the main length of cotton. Once all three colors of cotton have been twisted, lay them out side by side and gently twist them together. Fashion this multi-colored twist into a bracelet to wear or to give to Mom!

Fun Food to Fix:

Quick-as-a-Rabbit Rice Pudding

The Muslim Arabs also introduced sugar and rice to the West. Just think what it must have been like for the Europeans to get their first taste of sugar!

You will need: 1 cup cooked white rice; 1 package instant vanilla pudding ("Jell-O" brand works nicely); 2 cups cold milk (or whatever the package says for making the vanilla pudding)

Prepare the vanilla pudding according to the package directions, being sure to stir the pudding vigorously for a few minutes. Add the cooked rice, stirring well to blend in. It is best if you can let it sit for 30 minutes in the refrigerator. Enjoy!

Marvelous Mazes!

Islam went a long way in the first one hundred years it existed. Start in the center of the maze and try not to get confused as you follow each trail to discover just where the Islamic religion spread. Using markers of various colors might be fun here!

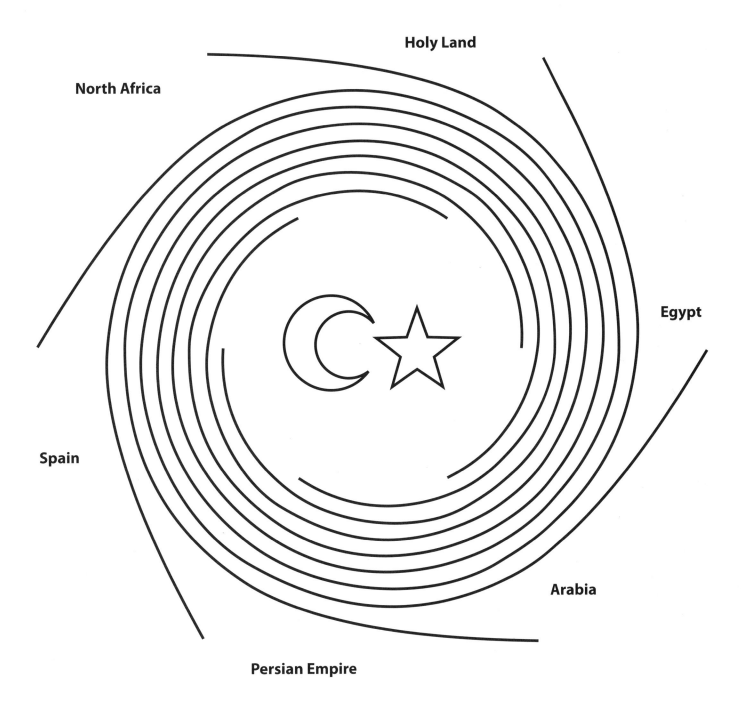

Your Own Masterpiece

Draw a picture depicting the Muslims attacking Constantinople.

Creative Fun with History!
Action Activity:

Invade & Defend

This game is designed to help students see how well Constantinople was protected against Muslim invasion.

Separate players into two teams. One team is the Byzantine Defenders (BD) and the other is the Muslim Invaders (MI). The BD players stand in a line, with their hands joined together—which represents the defenses Constantinople had in place—while the MI players stand opposite them.

All the BD players chant together:
"I'm by the Golden Horn, you see,
And no one yet can get past me!"

All the MI players chant together:
"Byzantines, Byzantines, You're not so great We are fierce Muslims, we'll break your gate!"

At this, one MI player runs across and tries to break through the line. If successful, the teams change places and play begins again. If unsuccessful, all the BD players chant together:

"We trust in God, we've built His church,
Our walls are strong, so go and search!"

All the MI players chant together:
"We have conquered where we've gone,
And pretty soon, you'll sing our song!"

At this, a different MI player runs across and tries to break through the line. If successful, the teams change places and play begins again. If unsuccessful, repeat the previous challenges until all the MI players have had a chance to break through the BD defenses. After all the MI players have tried unsuccessfully, all the BD players chant together:

"Constantinople is ours, so we'll fight,
Or throw Greek fire and make you light!"

All the MI players chant together:
"We are fierce Muslims, this is too hard,
We'll come again, when you're not on guard!"

At this, if the BD players have resisted all attacks, they are declared the winners. Feel free to rearrange teams and try again! If you are on an unsuccessful MI team, don't feel bad. It took the Muslims seven hundred years to successfully invade Constantinople!

The Holy Roman Empire & the Vikings

The Vikings

Bible Verses to Read & Talk About

God Takes Care of His People: Psalm 107:1–22

When the Vikings began to attack the British Isles and the coast of Europe, the cry of the Christians was, "From the Northmen, Good Lord, deliver us!" Read these scriptures and talk together about what this meant for the people during Viking times, and what it means to us today.

- For what reason should we give thanks to the Lord according to this psalm? Talk together about specific times in your life when God has done wonderful works.
- When did the Lord deliver His people out of their distresses? What can we learn from Psalm 107?

Suggested Books for Reading Together

How People Lived in the Middle Ages by Fred King & Herbert Epperly

Though written in somewhat of a textbook style, this little book is stuffed with interesting facts and pictures about the time of the Middle Ages.

Canterbury Tales, by Geoffrey Chaucer selected, translated, and adapted by Barbara Cohen

This is a delightful, well-illustrated adaptation of the tales of medieval people and events by Chaucer. This book makes a wonderful introduction for the whole family. It is a great read-aloud book.

Castle by David Macaulay

Imagine being able to see the process of building a medieval castle! This wonderfully informative book will be invaluable to you in understanding more about castles. Be sure to check out the video by the same title!

Knights in Armor—Living History edited by John Clare

This series of books is fascinating; they use real people to model historic costumes. This particular title shows suits of armor, battles, and feasting. If you have ever wondered how they got those suits on, this book will show you!

A Medieval Feast by Aliki

A medieval feast was not a casual snack thrown on the table! This book shows what kind of preparations were done for the visit of a king.

Kids in the Middle Ages by Lisa A. Wroble

For young children, a delightful primer on the Middle Ages.

Fascinating Folks & Exciting Events

Charlemagne, the First Holy Roman Emperor (742–814)

When barbarians invaded the western half of the Roman Empire, they set up rulers over the people of the land. Since there were so many different tribes who had conquered so many different places, there were lots and lots of rulers—but none of them ruled over a very large area! That all changed when Charles the Great (known as "Charlemagne") became king.

He was a very good warrior, which allowed him to conquer many places, and he was a very good ruler, which allowed the people under him to retain their own languages and customs. As Charlemagne conquered more regions and kingdoms, he built a new empire over the ashes of the old Roman Empire. Charlemagne was kneeling for prayer at church on Christmas Day, 800, when the pope brought a crown and placed it on his head, saying, "I crown you Holy Roman Emperor." Thus they created the Holy Roman Empire, which lasted 1,000 years until 1806!

Charlemagne wanted people to learn to read and write (he himself could read fairly well but never could get the hang of writing), so he brought the best teacher in Europe to set up schools in his palace. This excellent teacher's name was Alcuin. In Alcuin's school any student who was willing to work hard could come and study.

Charlemagne also encouraged art, music, literature, copying of manuscripts, and establishing libraries. However, the most important part of his rule was to encourage people to become Christians and then to live as Christian believers. His vision was for "Christendom" —Christian Roman Empire. This time period is known as the Carolingian Renaissance, and it had a tremendous influence on the Middle Ages.

The Vikings attack Europe & Feudalism is born (c. 793–1100)

While Charlemagne was uniting his empire in Europe, warriors from the northern lands of Scandinavia began looting the rich monasteries in the British Isles. These people from the North were called Vikings, and their warring raids, which began in the British Isles, changed the way people lived in France, Germany, Italy, and Spain! The cry of the Europeans for three hundred years was, "From the Northmen, Good Lord, deliver us!!"

The Vikings had such fast boats that they could appear suddenly and without warning to attack a town or village. They were such fierce warriors that isolated settlements had no hope of defending themselves. So, the various rulers of Europe decided to set up a system of military service, and that system led them to feudalism. In feudalism, a ruler would offer part of his land to someone if he would promise to give military service to the ruler for a certain number of days each year. The ruler was known as the "lord," and the person who accepted the land and gave the military service was known as the "vassal." Then that vassal would offer some of his newly received land to another person if he would promise to give military service for a certain number of days. This created another "lord" and another "vassal" (though this "lord" remained under the rule of his own "lord.") This continued on down through the ranks of people until it got to the poor people who farmed the land that everyone else owned. These poor farmers, called serfs, were tied to the land, which means they could not leave the land, and they were servants to the lord of the land. They farmed the land for the lord, only keeping a small portion for themselves, in exchange for military protection from the Vikings. Fortified castles, built by the lord, were the shelters everyone would run to for safety if the Vikings or other warring groups attacked.

The Vikings traveled to other places besides Europe. They set up colonies in Iceland, Greenland, and, for a brief time, in North America! They also traveled down through Russia (which got its name from the Swedes) to trade in Constantinople, and even as far as Baghdad! As the Vikings traveled to these far-flung places, they often settled down and became farmers and merchants. So, you see, the Vikings were not always fierce raiders who destroyed places— though the Europeans of their day would have certainly disagreed!

Word Search

Using the words from your vocabulary list at the bottom of the page, search for words in the puzzle. The words are diagonal, vertical, and horizontal. Have fun!

```
Q T E F Y U S K E S C F K P W X I E J
B D C D A M A E T E F C N L R I M G F
C H A P E L N C A R B U I G I L S R N
H C S R G P J S L F H R G E F B N E B
A D T L Y N O M B A A X H V G N E E F
R S L H W D U S C T R R T O J F S N O
L G E P Q G S T E D V Y E M P H G L L
E G U H C S T F A M J A H R T P O A K
M I R I Y Z E H L N P C D A S K V N E
A L F R E D H L O A W H T N R A I D X
G V Y T E E R I R I A I K T Y I K R I
N A S P D F E U D A L P N T M G I H S
E S P M H E O I W T R E A T Y H N A F
F S P C L A C R R P O A O T L T G D N
J A R B S T N P M O M R O L L O S R R
T L O H G K P T G E V T N A T L E A J
O Q I E E L A N D G E M L H T F L K P
```

Alfred	castle	chapel	Charlemagne	defeat	depose	feudal
Greenland	Iceland	joust	knight	lord	reform	Rollo
raid	seafarers	serf	treaty	vassal	Vikings	

Hands-On History Fun
Create-A-Craft:

Build a replica of Charlemagne's Palace

Using empty boxes you have available and your imagination, make a simple replica of part of Charlemagne's beautiful castle at Aachen (in Germany).

> **You will need: Empty boxes and tubes, such as boxes from oatmeal, paper towels, tissues, toothpaste, cake mix; Tempera paint—white, or whatever color you prefer; Sections of egg carton cut apart; Large piece of cardboard for the base; Construction paper; Scissors; Tape; Glue; Spray paint for stone walls; Marking pens; Sponge cut into 1 inch squares**

Try making the various parts as illustrated below, attach them to each other with tape, then fasten them with glue or tape to the cardboard base.

Here are some suggestions:

- For the rounded roof: use one piece of construction paper. Draw and cut out a circle on the paper. Fold the circle in half, fold it in half again, then fold it in half once more. Unfold the circle of paper. There should be eight sections made by the folding action. Using the scissors, cut out two of the sections (side by side). Now bring the cut edges together and tape them to form a six-sided dome that will sit on the top of the empty, round oatmeal box. Tape or glue it to the round box.

- To create towers: use individual pieces of egg carton (the part that would hold one egg) to sit on top of the paper towel tube or the toothpaste box (or one of each).

- To make a building with a sloping roof: use a half piece of construction paper, fold it in half, and set it on top of two cake mix boxes. Use tape or glue to hold the roof in place. Make a cross for the top of a building: cut out a small cross shape from an empty box, then tape it to the top of a tall rectangular box.

CAUTION: ADULT SUPERVISION REQUIRED. When the castle is completed, carefully take it outside to an appropriate site for spray painting. Follow the directions on the can of paint. Your castle will probably need several light coats of paint. After the castle has dried, you may want to use sponge pieces and tempera to paint "stones" on the castle walls. Use the markers to draw windows and doors.

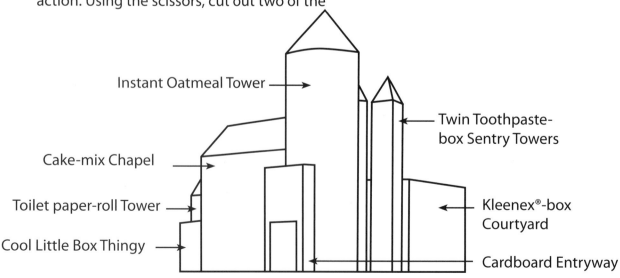

Instant Oatmeal Tower

Twin Toothpaste-box Sentry Towers

Cake-mix Chapel

Toilet paper-roll Tower

Cool Little Box Thingy

Kleenex®-box Courtyard

Cardboard Entryway

Where in the World . . .

is Scandinavia?

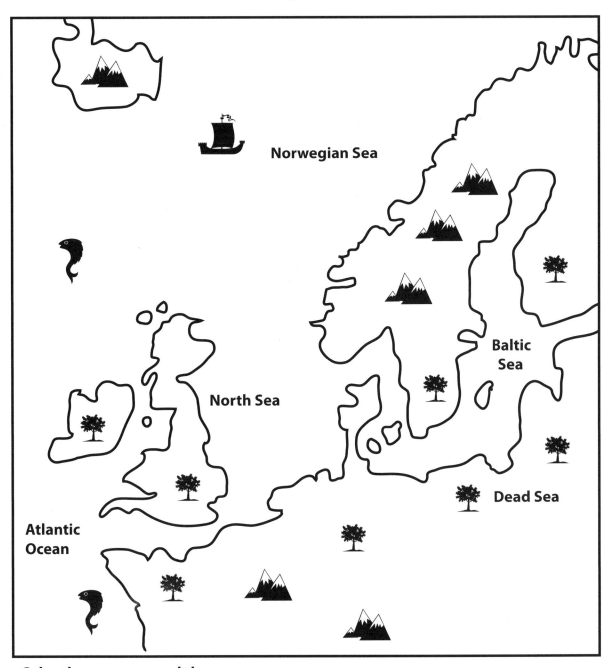

Color the areas around these:

 purple mountains

green vegetation

 blue water

Clues for finding Scandinavia:

- I am SOUTH of the Norwegian Sea.
- I am EAST of the North Sea.

- I am NORTH and WEST of the Baltic Sea.

Where am I?

Your Own Masterpiece

Draw a picture of King Alfred burning the peasant woman's cakes.

Creative Fun with History!
Acting Up History:

The Story of King Alfred versus The Danes

Narrator:
A wondrous tale I've come to tell
About a king of old.
And, by the time my story's done,
On Alfred, you'll be sold!
In Alfred's day, old England gained
A navy, boats and such.
They even won a victory
At sea! A master touch!!

Chorus: (pointing in time to Alfred)
Alfred, Alfred, he's our man.
If he can't win, then no one can!

King Alfred:
Ahem. Thank you... (He stands to recite)
The Danes had come to steal our land
To kill, and loot, and burn.
We had to find a way to win
But quick! We had to learn.
The Danes, they came in Viking boats
And more, yet more, still more!
We fought them oft' in battles great
'Til all our folks were sore.
I had to flee to forests deep
And live upon the land,
Waiting for the proper time
My army to command.

Narrator:
Far away from spying eyes,
King Alfred comes to rest.
A peasant man and wife invite
Him in to be their guest.

Chorus: (pointing to Woman in the Hut)
She is the Woman in the Hut
(pointing in time at Alfred)
She thinks HE is some kind of nut!

Woman in the Hut:
I asked this guest to mind the cakes
A-cooking with the heat.

And while I turns to do my work,
He burns them black as peat!
HUMPH!! (she turns her back on Alfred)

Chorus: (pointing to Alfred)
Alfred, dear, don't feel the sting,
(pointing to the Woman in the Hut)
She doesn't know that you're the king!

Narrator:
King Alfred played the harp and sang
His songs quite well, you know.
So Guthrum, leader of the Danes,
Once said, "Come, do a show!"
Chorus: (pointing in time to Guthrum)
Guthrum, Guthrum, can't you see
That singer is your enemy!

Guthrum:
I asked a traveling man to play
His harp, with songs to sing.
I didn't have the slightest clue
He was the Saxon King!

Alfred:
When Guthrum brought me to his camp,
He little knew the cost.
I learned how best to beat the Danes
And so, you see, they lost!
At end of battle, Guthrum came
A beaten man, my slave.
He saw the "singer" was the king.
I spoke, and thus forgave.
"Dear Sir, if you will promise me
You'll never fight again,
And be a Christian from now on,
You'll see, we can be friends!"

Narrator:
So, Guthrum and his group obeyed,
And soon were all baptized.
They never fought the king again!
Now say, are you surprised?

UNIT 5

The Crusades
& the Mongols

Marco Polo

Bible Verses to Read & Talk About

God's Way, Not Man's Way: Matthew 26:51–52; Romans 10:8–15, 12:18–21; Philippians 4:4–9

When Pope Urban II called for the First Crusade against the Muslims in the Holy Land, the European knights and rulers went as soldiers bent on conquest and destruction. They did this under the banner of the Cross of Christ, as a "Christian Army," with the cry, "Deus Veult," which means "God wills it."

- When you read these Scriptures together, talk about the differences between what God tells us our actions and attitudes should be toward people of different beliefs (like Muslims), and what the Crusaders' actions and attitudes were when they went to the Holy Land.

- During the time of the Crusades, there were few Bibles available since each one had to be copied by hand. Because of this, most people probably did not know these Scriptures. How would people have behaved differently if they had been able to read the Bible?

Suggested Books & Videos for the Whole Family

Famous Men of the Middle Ages by John H. Haaren & A. B. Poland

Included in this unit for its clear and valuable biographies of this time period. Highly recommended!

Genghis Khan and the Mongol Horde by Harold Lamb

This well written biography describes the young Temujin who becomes more and more powerful in uniting the Mongols, eventually ruling much of the world. This is a great read-aloud story for all ages.

Richard the Lionheart and the Crusades—Life and Times by Christopher Gibb

This is an excellent book filled with facts and with pictures of Richard I of England. He was one of the leaders of the Third Crusade and was a very important warrior of his time period. Actually, he was so busy warring, that he only spent about six months of his ten-year reign in England!

Robin Hood (Video) by Disney

Though it is a cartoon, this is a wonderful way to learn history. Talk with your children about King Richard being gone to the Third Crusade and about the effect upon England of having Prince John in charge!

Fascinating Folks & Exciting Events

Marco Polo (1254–1324)

When Marco was six years old, his father and uncle left on a merchant's journey to the Crimea. When they had finished their business, they discovered that a tremendous war was raging across their homeward route, so they decided to go forward, across the desert, past Central Asia until they found themselves in China. There in China, or "Cathay" as it was known, they met the great Kublai Khan, the Mongol emperor over the Chinese. He wanted to know all about Europe, especially about Rome and the Christian faith. The Khan requested that the Polo brothers return to Europe and ask the Pope to send one hundred teachers who could teach the Chinese about Christianity! When the Polo brothers returned home (Marco was now fifteen years old), they found that the Pope had died and no one had been appointed in his place. After waiting for two years, they decided to return to the Khan and tell him their mission had failed. Marco was allowed to go with them.

Thus began a journey of many years to many faraway places. It took three and a half years just to get to China! Once there, Marco began studying the Chinese language and becoming familiar with their customs. The Khan was impressed with this young man and began sending him on diplomatic missions throughout the Empire. For seventeen years, the three Polos worked for the Khan, having amazing experiences and seeing incredible sights. However, they knew that they needed to leave China before the Khan died, since the next ruler might not be so friendly toward the Polo family! The Khan did not want to let them go. In fact, he told them that it hurt his feelings to have them even request such a thing. An opportunity came at last when a princess of the court was betrothed to a Persian prince. The princess had to travel to Persia by water since there was a war taking place along the overland route.

The people in charge of the journey begged the Khan to let the Polos travel with them because they were from a sea-faring people and understood navigation better than anyone else. The Khan reluctantly granted permission for them to leave. Their journey to Persia took two years! After yet another year of travel, they arrived home to Venice.

It was the year 1295, and the Polos had been gone for twenty-four years. People did not recognize them since they looked so strange in their foreign dress and because they were constantly speaking to each other in Chinese. But, when they ripped open the lining of their tattered coats and out poured jewels of all kinds—more than had ever been seen in Venice—folks were convinced! Shortly after that, Marco was in a sea battle and was captured and thrown into a Genoese prison. To make the time pass more quickly, he told his adventures to a fellow prisoner who wrote it all down. Marco Polo's travels were captured on paper and distributed throughout Europe. His account helped people to know more about Asia and the Far East, though they could hardly believe what they read!

Pigpen Puzzle

The key provided near the bottom shows the code—the alphabet placed within special shapes. Your vocabulary words are spelled out in the Pigpen Puzzle, but only the code shapes are given. You must decode each line by supplying the letter that belongs in each code shape. The symbols without dots represent the letters A–M; the symbols with dots represent the letters N–Z.

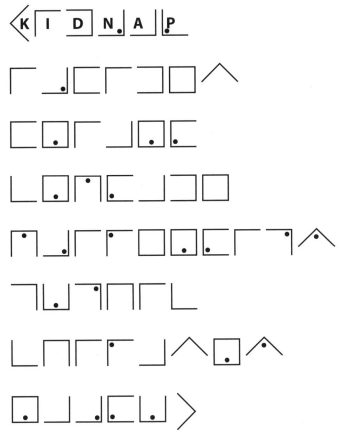

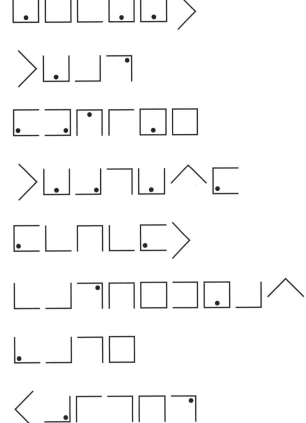

cathedral   chivalry   crusade   friars   gothic   infidel

~~kidnap~~   knight   moat   Mongols   page   ransom

reform   schism   squire   university

Hands-On History Fun
Create-a-Craft:

Stained Glass Window

You will need: black crayon; other colors of crayon; cotton ball; vegetable oil

You will need to make a photocopy of the following picture in order to create the stained glass window. Use the black crayon to outline this picture. Then, color in each separate portion with pretty crayon colors (bright colors work best). When you are finished, dip a cotton ball into a small amount of vegetable oil and brush lightly over the picture. Let it dry, then hang it up in a sunny window. Beautiful! You could also make your own picture.

Fun Food to Fix:

Ginger Snaps

The folks who went on the Crusades brought back stories of incredible spices in the East. That started a huge business of bringing spices to Europe from the East to satisfy the new taste buds of Europeans. Just think how boring it would be if we did not have yummy spices to use in these cookies!

You will need: 1 cup margarine or butter; 1 cup brown sugar; 1 cup molasses; 1 tablespoon apple cider vinegar; 1 large egg; 2 teaspoons ginger; 5 cups sifted flour; 2 teaspoons baking powder; ½ teaspoon salt; 1 teaspoon cinnamon; 1 teaspoon cloves

CAUTION: ADULT SUPERVISION REQUIRED. In a saucepan, combine the margarine (or butter), brown sugar, molasses, and apple cider vinegar. Heat and stir just until the margarine melts. Take off the heat and cool until lukewarm. While this cools, sift together the flour, baking powder, and spices. Beat the egg, then add it to the cooled margarine/sugar mixture. Add the sifted flour mixture and stir until it is well combined. Roll dough on a lightly floured surface. Using cookie cutters, cut out different shapes (like gingerbread men, trees, etc.). Grease a baking tin and carefully place the cookies on it. Bake it at 350 degrees for about 10 minutes. Watch them carefully so they don't scorch! Cool on racks and glaze or decorate as desired. YUM!

Marvelous Mazes!

Travel with King Richard the Lionhearted on his crusade to the Holy Land. Don't take a wrong turn or you'll hit a dead end!

Your Own Masterpiece

Draw a picture of a crusader on horseback.

Creative Fun with History!

Rhyme Time:

Choose one person to be "Marco Polo." Line up all the other players across the room from Marco Polo. Decide on an order of turns, such as youngest-to-oldest, or shortest-to-tallest. The players will take turns making a rhyme, like those listed below. (When a rhyme is used, it is then taken out of play until there is a new Marco Polo. The more people playing, the more rhymes you will have to learn!)

As a player says a rhyme, he must make an appropriate action to go with the rhyme. If he makes an appropriate action when a rhyme is said, then Marco Polo must say, "Yay, I say, Yay. Yes, you may!" and the player takes one step forward. If the player fails to make an appropriate action while saying the rhyme, then Marco Polo will say, "Nay, I say, Nay. Sta-ay-ay," and the player must remain in the same spot. When a player reaches Marco Polo, a winner is declared, and the winner becomes the next Marco Polo.

Note: You may make up your own rhymes, but they must follow the rhythm pattern of the rhymes below.

Marco Polo,
      Shall I bow low, yes/no?

Marco Polo,
      May I go-go, yes/no?

Marco Polo,
      Must I tiptoe, yes/no?

Marco Polo,
      Should I walk slow, yes/no?

Marco Polo,
      Play the oboe, yes/no?

Marco Polo,
      See the rainbow, yes/no?

Marco Polo,
      Is that cold snow, yes/no?

Marco Polo,
      Strum the banjo, yes/no?

Marco Polo,
      May I make dough, yes/no?

Marco Polo,
      Shall I tall grow, yes/no?

The Seeds of Reformation

& the Late Middle Ages

John Wycliffe

Bible Verses to Read & Talk About

Living as a Disciple of Jesus, Not as a Lordly Ruler over Others: Matthew 23:1–12, Luke 9:57–58, Philippians 3:8–14

During the late Middle Ages, the leaders of the Catholic Church lived in great splendor and luxury with much earthly power, as the emperors and kings did. This caused many people to question whether these leaders truly represented Christianity. Read these scriptures and discuss together whether the Church in the Middle Ages was obedient or disobedient to the Word of God.

- In the passage in Matthew, what does Jesus say about the greatest person among you? What will happen to the one who humbles himself/herself? What do you think this means? Describe some ways you can do this in your family.

- Luke 9:57–58 describes Jesus's earthly home during His ministry. What does He say about it? Why do you think Jesus, the Son of God, didn't have a big palace or mansion to live in while He was on earth? What were the most important things to Him? Do you think these are important for us to consider in our own lives? Why or why not?

- Read Philippians 3:8–14. What does Paul indicate is his greatest desire? To learn more about the life Paul lived after he became a Christian, read together 2 Corinthians 11:24–28. What do you think Paul would have said about living in palaces with great luxury and power?

Suggested Books for Reading Together

Ink on His Fingers by Louise A. Vernon

This is the story of Gutenberg and the printing of the first Bible. Very enjoyable!

The Door in the Wall by Marguerite de Angeli

A story of a young boy in "olde England" who perseveres through what seem to him to be insurmountable obstacles to continue serving his king. It is set during the time of the Scottish wars. A wonderful tale, and a Newberry Award winner, as well.

Fascinating Folks & Exciting Events

John Wycliffe (c. 1329–1384)

Born in the north of England, John Wycliffe was known as one of the great scholars of the age. He taught at Oxford University when it was quite new. As he studied and taught, he became more and more concerned about differences between the truth in the Bible and the traditions of the Catholic Church. So, he began to publicly speak out and write pamphlets about issues, such as the wealth and luxury of the popes, the sale of indulgences (which they said allowed a person to get out of "purgatory" sooner), pilgrimages to holy places, and other things. Wycliffe believed that all of our doctrines and actions needed to line up with the Bible—beliefs which later reformers, like Martin Luther, followed during the Reformation. He also held that each believer could have a personal relationship with God without needing a priest, bishop, or pope in between.

These are the reasons Wycliffe is called the "Morning Star of the Reformation." But, perhaps, John Wycliffe is best known for his translation of the Bible from Latin into English. This was important so that the common people would be able to hear the Bible in their mother tongue. He gathered a number of scholars at Oxford to help him make this English translation—the first ever—and then sent out "poor preachers" to read the Bible and teach Christian doctrine to the people. One writer of the time remarked that every second person he met was one of Wycliffe's poor preachers! Thirty-one years after John Wycliffe died, he was condemned by the Catholic Church as a heretic. However, England and many other nations of Europe owe a tremendous debt to John Wycliffe for his courageous work.

Prince Henry the Navigator (1394–1460)

Henry was a prince in the country of Portugal at a time when Europeans believed that if you sailed too far south, monstrous sea dragons would eat you up, or boiling seas would cook you dead, or evil demons would snatch you! It's not hard to understand why ships stayed fairly close to home. Prince Henry, though, was a devout man and not superstitious, so he wanted to know more. He wanted to know whether it were possible to get over to the Indies and China by going down the coast of Africa. He wanted to find possible allies in a holy war against the Muslims. He wanted his country to stop paying exorbitant prices to the Muslim middlemen who brought Oriental goods to the Europeans. And, because he was a prince, he was able to give it a go!

He hired lots and lots of sailors, navigators, scientists, map-makers, astronomers, and more. His sailing captains were told to sail south of Cape Bojador (the bulge on the west coast of Africa, just south of the Canary Islands), but whenever they reached that spot, panic would set in. Back the terrified sailors would go to Portugal and Prince Henry. He would patiently and sternly tell them to try again . . . and again . . . and again. However, one stout-hearted young captain managed to sail past the scary spot—by sailing away from the coast and out to sea! When folks realized that nothing ate the ship nor boiled the crew, they became a little more courageous. Little by little, voyage by voyage, they sailed farther along the coast of Africa. Thus began the incredible "Age of Exploration."

Cypher Wheel

Photocopy this page, and then cut out the two circles. Punch a hole through the center in the middle of the circle, then insert a brad to hold the two together, the smaller one in front. If A=D, then place the smaller circle so that the D lines up under the bigger circle's A, then decode the letters one by one!

- If you set your Cypher Wheel so that A=G, then "Africa" would look like this: Glxoig

- If you set your Cypher Wheel so that A=P, then "barons" would look like this: qpgdch

- How would "truce" look if A=Y?

- Or if A=D?

- If P=M, which vocabulary word would look like this: phufkdqw?

Try writing some more vocabulary words in your own Cypher Wheel Code! See if your parents or brothers and sisters can decode them.

Africa	barons	breach	cave	commerce
explore	fair	guild	Gutenberg	Hundred Years War
long bow	merchant	navigator	plague	printing
revenue	town	trade	truce	John Wycliffe

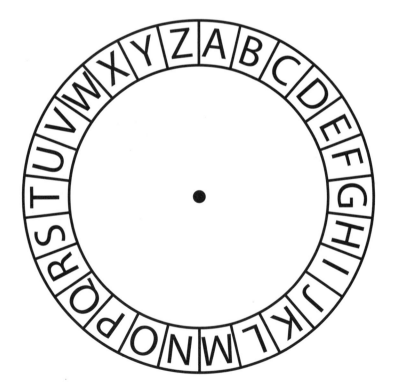

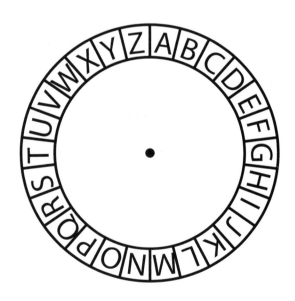

Hands-On History Fun
Create- A-Craft:

Twisted Yarn Belt

If you had lived in Europe during the late Middle Ages, you would have seen something astonishing and new: Trading Fairs! Merchants from many places came to an area of France known as Champagne to sell wonderful items from around the world. One of the most exciting products for the visitors at the fair was the beautiful fabric being created in Flanders (in modern day Belgium). Try your hand at creating this great belt and decide whether you would have been able to sell it at the fair.

> **You will need, for each belt maker: 4 strands of yarn, each 9 feet long (the thicker and knobbier the better!); scissors**

Holding all four strands of yarn together, tie a knot at each end. You will need two people to work together for the next part. Have each person hold one knot and then stand far enough apart that the yarn is straight and fairly taut. Each person then begins turning his or her end of the yarn clockwise, which will create twists in the yarn. Keep turning the yarn until it starts to "kink" or until no more twists can be put into the yarn.

Now, holding the yarn straight, have one person give his or her knot to the other person. Hold those two knots together, let go of the rest of the yarn, and watch the two parts wind around each other! If there are any loops, just smooth them out toward an end. Tie a knot around each end to secure the twist. One end will already have loose "fringe." Using the scissors, cut the loops on the other end to have fringe on both ends.

Fun Food to Fix:

Chocolate "Moose" (Normally spelled "mousse")

During the time period of the late Middle Ages, the pope moved his "court" from Rome to the south of France. The city he lived in is called "Avignon" (pronounced "av-een-yon").

French cooking is some of the most wonderful in the world. Here is a simplified-for-children recipe for one of the most beloved French desserts.

> **You will need: 2 packages instant chocolate pudding; 2 cups milk; 1 teaspoon vanilla; 1 cup whipping cream (or whipped topping, such as Cool Whip, if you prefer)**

Make the pudding according to the directions on the package. Add the vanilla. Let the pudding set for five to ten minutes. Beat the cream until it is stiff (CAUTION: If you beat cream TOO long, it turns to butter!). Carefully stir the whipped cream into the chocolate pudding until it is well-blended. If you don't eat the "moose" immediately, refrigerate it until just before serving. Oo-la-la!

Where in the World . . .
is Africa?

Color the areas around these:

purple mountains

green vegetation

blue water

yellow desert

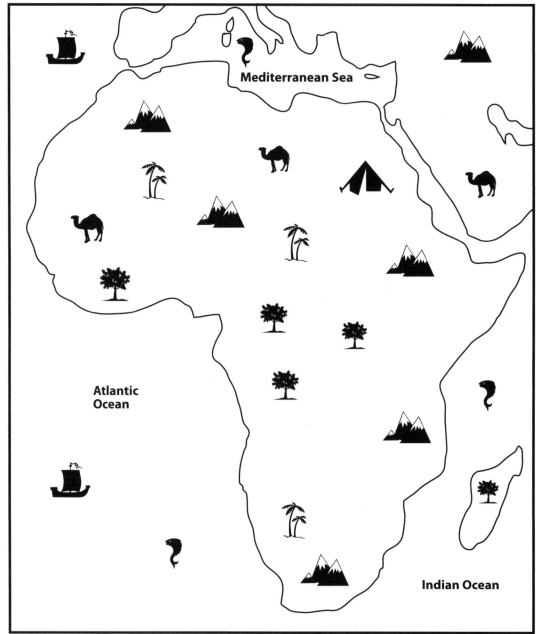

Mediterranean Sea

Atlantic Ocean

Indian Ocean

Clues for finding Africa:

- I am EAST of the Atlantic Ocean.
- I am SOUTH of the Mediterranean Sea.
- I am made up of a continent and an island in the Indian Ocean on my SOUTHEASTERN side.

Where am I?

Your Own Masterpiece

Draw a picture of Prince Henry's ships sailing down the coast of Africa.

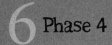

Creative Fun with History!
Singing Somewhat Silly Songs:

Oh, Gutenberg, Sir! (to the tune of "Oh, Susanna")

Oh, in the Middle Ages,
The books were writ by hand
Upon the skins of critters—ICK!
The rich thought it was grand.

The poor, they had no choices, No
books for them to read,
But a wondrous work was coming,
Their wishes to exceed!

Chorus:
Oh, Gutenberg, Sir!
Oh, won't you print for me?
For I want to read the Bible and
Be part of history!

Some tried to make books faster
By inking blocks of wood.
They would carve each page on one block,
Print it out as best they could.

But to print a book or Bible
Was far more than they could do.
With so very many pages,
They just couldn't make it through!

Chorus

Then a German man named Johann
Tried a very different way,
Using separate metal letters
That could move without delay!

So he formed some words together
Line by line and page by page.
With some printer's ink and paper,
Printed books were soon the rage!

Chorus

Now, the Bible was the first book
That Johann printed through.
So the people all could have one Thanks
to Johann, so can you!

The Renaissance & the Reformation

Martin Luther

Bible Verses to Read & Talk About

Living by Faith in the Son of God: Habakkuk 2:4, Romans 1:17, Galatians 2:16, Ephesians 2:8–10

Martin Luther was amazed when he discovered what the Bible had to say concerning our relationship with God—that it was not by our own work and merit. Read these Scriptures together and talk about what they mean to you.

- Where does salvation come from? How do we receive it? Do we have to earn our salvation? Why or why not?

What God Has Done for Us: 2 Corinthians 5:20–21, Colossians 1:19–20

- Who makes us right with God? How do we receive His righteousness? What does "reconcile" mean? Talk together about where our right standing with God comes from.

The Importance of the Scriptures: 2 Timothy 3:15–17, Hebrews 4:12

The Reformation came about as people like Martin Luther began reading the Bible and believing what it said, even if it contradicted long-held traditions of the church. Read these Scriptures together and talk about the place of the Bible in our beliefs.

- Who is the source of Scripture in our Bible? What does Scripture do for us?

Suggested Books for Reading Together

Famous Men of the Renaissance & Reformation by Robert Shearer

This is a wonderful introduction to the people of this time period. Rob Shearer has done an excellent job of describing such people as Lorenzo de Medici, Michelangelo, John Wycliffe, Martin Luther, and many more. Highly recommended!

The Man Who Laid the Egg by Louise A. Vernon

This is the story of the early reformer, Erasmus, the man of whom the monks said, "Erasmus laid the egg that Luther hatched." It is written as historical fiction for children. Find wonderful insight into this fascinating time. Great for read-aloud!

Thunderstorm in Church by Louise A. Vernon

The story of Martin Luther is told in this book through the use of historical fiction. Another great read-aloud!

Spy for the Night Riders: Martin Luther by Dave & Neta Jackson

One of the Trailblazer books, this is a great story for elementary age students. It takes us back to the University of Wittenberg in 1520, as well as the Diet of Worms. A can't-put-it-down book!

The Queen's Smuggler: William Tyndale by Dave & Neta Jackson

Another Trailblazer title, this is the exciting story of "God's Smuggler" during the 1500s. William Tyndale, who was an English martyr, had a tremendous impact on the Church in England. Well worth reading.

The Betrayer's Fortune: Menno Simons by Dave & Neta Jackson

A story of the Anabaptists during the mid-1500s; a wonderful book. Reading the Trailblazer series is kind of like eating potato chips—"bet you can't read just one!" We love them.

Kids During the Renaissance by Lisa A. Wroble

This is a fun little book for your young children, showing much of the day-to-day living during the time of the Renaissance.

Fascinating Folks & Exciting Events

Christopher Columbus (1451–1506)

This very famous man was the son of a poor Italian weaver. Christopher Columbus, while still a very young man, decided to follow his dreams and became a sailor on the high seas. When his ship was wrecked during a sea battle off the coast of Portugal in 1476, he decided to remain in Lisbon and learn the art of mapmaking. This did not destroy his love for the sea! He sailed to England, and even to Iceland, where he may have heard stories about Viking adventurers sailing west and finding land.

With an insatiable curiosity, Columbus studied books, interviewed sailors, considered maps, and eventually came to the startling conclusion that one could get to Asia by sailing west. He sought royal sponsors who could pay for this Asian-bound voyage to the west, but it was a long and difficult search. In 1492 Queen Isabella of Spain finally agreed to finance Columbus's journey. Thus, "in fourteen ninety-two, Columbus sailed the ocean blue!" After several tension-filled weeks at sea, the terrified sailors spotted land. Thinking that they had sailed to Asia and India, Columbus called the native people of the islands "Indians." It wasn't until his third journey that Columbus realized his mistake—that he had actually found the New World! The rest, as they say, is history.

Martin Luther (1483–1546)

The German reformer Martin Luther was one of the most earth-shaking people in history. He was educated as a law student, but, after narrowly escaping with his life from a terrible storm, he decided to become a monk. In his duties as a monk, Luther kept trying to do enough good things to be acceptable to God, but he knew it was hopeless. Then one day, while he was reading the New Testament in Greek, he read "the just shall live by faith." With a blinding light of revelation, Luther understood that it was by faith in the Son of God and His sacrificial death, rather than in good deeds, that a person would be justified before God.

This personal insight became public knowledge when, on October 31, 1517, Martin Luther nailed 95 "theses" (or arguments) on the door of the Wittenberg Cathedral. He was challenging many of the traditions of the Catholic Church, which were founded in men's ideas, rather than in the Bible. When church officials demanded that Luther publicly change his mind, he refused with this statement, "My conscience is captive to the Word of God . . . Here I stand, I can do no other."

Though he was condemned for his views, friends were able to keep him hidden at a lonely castle until it was safe. During his long stay at the castle, Luther began working on a translation of the Greek New Testament into the German language of the day. He wrote in a style that was not stiff and formal, but more the way people really converse, which made the Bible much easier for them to understand. Eventually, after he was free again, he married and had six children.

Along with the other things Luther wrote, he also wrote hymns using the tunes from familiar songs so that the people would be able to sing about God and His ways. One of the best known of these hymns is "A Mighty Fortress is Our God." His writings about reforming the Church (as well as his translation of the Bible) were printed and distributed throughout Europe, thanks to the recent invention of the printing press. Many people were convinced that Luther's ideas were right, and his efforts started what we call the Reformation.

Word Search

Using the words from your vocabulary list at the bottom of the page, search for words in the puzzle. The words are diagonal, vertical, and horizontal. Have fun!

```
P F A T R L E Q M O R E A P H W A B S D E T
O R E N A I S S A N C E O N E T G I A C O A
R A O S H E Y A C L E S C O R T E Z T Y U S
T U M T M B L E I S W M I N E E O A R E L P
U N L M E V E S R T W A R W T O F U N D U S
G G R E E S W H C I Z G A Y I E E O H A T N
A F E A W A T J U S T E Y W C E X G O D H I
L G F R G I N A M I U L P G O L P D L A E S
M I O R M F I S N E T L I T C E L B U E R G
U Y R S C A O O A T B A Y I O S O A D O G W
H O M I S C N S V H A N L G M E R I T G Y O
R P A T R O N Y I A T L E Y P S A T H I S M
A N T I S L K I G M N D A F A I T H K N O H
T I I M E U A N A H O B A D S L I E T T E R
T H O I S M T H T E S O R O S W O H E R S E
M Y N A M B I M E C K S R A A T N A S I P N
F C O N Q U I S T A D O R S E A N K E I A S
L O S E L S I K X A F E L T A B H O S E I N
T H G R E A D N G R B A L B O A E E N O N T
```

Age of Exploration	Balboa	circumnavigate	Columbus	compass
conquistadors	Cortez	faith	Germany	heretic
Italy	just	Luther	Magellan	merit
Moors	patron	Portugal	Protestant	Reformation
Renaissance	Spain			

Hands-On History Fun!

Create-A-Craft:

Create three dimensional objects with homemade modeling dough

Michelangelo was one of the greatest artists of the Renaissance. He painted the ceiling of the Sistine Chapel in Rome—while lying on his back! However, Michelangelo is best remembered for his amazing sculptures. For inspiration, see if you can find pictures of some of his sculptures, especially the *Pieta*.

You will need: 1 cup salt; ½ cup cornstarch; ²/₃ cup water; Various colors of food coloring

Mix the salt, cornstarch and water, and cook over low heat, stirring constantly until the mixture thickens. Remove from heat and allow to cool. Divide the dough into two or three portions and knead in your choice of food colorings. Now, begin creating your sculpture! You may wish to make an animal, a rock, trees, or other objects from nature. Let your creation air-dry and then show it to your friends and family!

Fun Food to Fix:

Italian Ice

Italy was the land where the Renaissance began. Excellent scholars from the Byzantine Empire fled to Italy when Constantinople was taken by the Muslims in 1453. Their knowledge of Greek and Roman literature, philosophy, history, science, etc., was fascinating to the people of Europe. This is what ignited the "Renaissance." Renaissance means "rebirth," and this was a rebirth of ancient knowledge.

You will need: 2 cups water; 1 cup sugar; 1 cup fruit juice (lemon, orange, pineapple, etc.)

CAUTION: ADULT SUPERVISION REQUIRED. On top of the stove, bring the water and sugar to a boil over medium heat, stirring constantly until the sugar dissolves. Set a timer for five minutes once the mixture begins to boil. At the end of five minutes, remove the sugar-water from the stove. Cool. Stir in the fruit juice, then pour into a shallow plastic bowl. Place the bowl in the freezer. Freeze the mixture for about four hours, stirring occasionally. Serve while very cold and thick. Yummy!

Marvelous Mazes!

Set sail with the Portugese explorer Ferdinand Magellan on his journey to the Spice Islands. He was the first explorer to attempt to reach them by sailing WEST instead of east from Europe.

Your Own Masterpiece

Draw a picture of Martin Luther pinning his 95 theses to the church door.

Creative Fun with History!

Acting Up History:

Henry the Eight-th & The Strife That He Made-th

Cast: Narrator; King Henry VIII; Queen Catherine; People on the street

Narrator:
In England of old,
Folks did what was told,
And the king was the top of the heap.
What he wanted he got,
To deny him was not
The best way to live long and sleep deep!

Henry VIII: (in a grumpy voice)
I don't like that Luther.
I don't like him, NO!
(with his arms folded)
He ought to be stopped!
I would fierce tell him so.

People on the Street:
(nodding their heads in approval)
Uh-huh. Yes. Uh-huh. We see.
Uh-huh. Yes. Uh-huh. Agree.

Narrator:
For this attitude,
We should all conclude,
"Defender of Faith" he was named.
The pope thought him grand;
Felt he took quite a stand.
So this honor was quickly acclaimed.

Henry VIII: (in a grumpy voice)
I don't like that Catherine.
I don't like her, NO!
(with his arms folded)
She really should leave!
I would fierce tell her so.

People on the Street:
(shaking their heads in disapproval)
Mm-mm. No. Mm-mm. Don't see.
Mm-mm. No. Mm-mm. Don't agree.

Queen Catherine:
Henry, my dear,
You can't send me away.

I'm rightfully queen
And here I will stay!
(points to the ground)

People on the Street:
(nodding their heads in approval)
Uh-huh. Yes. Uh-huh. We see.
Uh-huh. Yes. Uh-huh. Agree.

Narrator:
But Henry liked Anne,
And he quick made a plan -
To proclaim he had wrongly been wed.
So he pleaded to Rome,
"Send Catherine home!
"And I'll marry Anne rightly instead."
But the pope said, "No."

Henry VIII: (in a grumpy voice)
I don't like the pope's words.
I don't like them, NO!
(with his arms folded)
I'll do what I want to!
I would fierce tell him so.

People on the Street: (half the group says)
Uh-huh. Yes. Uh-huh. We see.
Uh-huh. Yes. Uh-huh. Agree.
(at the same time, the other half says)
Mm-mm. No. Mm-mm. Don't see.
Mm-mm. No. Mm-mm. Don't agree.

Narrator:
A group soon was sent
To become Parliament
And to issue a divorce decree.
They did what he asked
And completed their task.
Reformation of England, you see.
Now our tale is told
'Bout England of old
And how Protestant she came to be.
King Henry the Eight-th
And the strife that he made-th
Are all part of the world's history!

Puritans, Pietists, & the Divine Right of Kings

Galileo

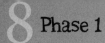

Bible Verses to Read & Talk About

Where We Put Our Trust: Psalm 16:1–3, Psalm 34:1–8, Philippians 3:4–11

In the mid-1600s, a Frenchman named Blaise Pascal had a dramatic effect on the thinking of many French people. He wrote several public "letters" against the teachings of some very prominent teachers because they were counseling people to trust in their own good works for salvation. Read these Scripture passages together and talk about what you learn.

- When you read these Psalms, who is the one being described as good? Who is the one who delivers and saves? In whom should we put our trust?

- List the things Paul says were important to him before. What does he say about them now? What is the most important thing Paul names now?

A Matter of the Heart: Matthew 15: 7–9

In Germany, during this same time frame, a group of people known as Pietists began meeting. They were very concerned that Christianity had become merely a matter of rules and regulations, doctrines, and church attendance. They believed that each person needs to have a personal, experiential relationship with Jesus Christ. Read this Scripture passage together and talk about what you learn.

- In the passage in Matthew, how does Jesus describe people who "talk the talk" but don't have it in their heart? What does that mean for us today?

Suggested Books for Reading Together

1620: Year of the Pilgrims by Genevieve Foster

This wonderful book covers not only the Pilgrims, but also Shakespeare, Rembrandt, Galileo, Akbar of India, and more. Highly recommended!

The World of William Penn by Genevieve Foster

A great book for younger students, this one covers the years 1660–1718. Highly recommended!

Sir Francis Drake by Roy Gerrard

Though this is a delightful picture book for younger students, it is a fantastic and hilarious description of Drake's adventures in poetry form!

Elizabeth I and Tudor England: Life and Times by Stephen White-Thomson

Great book for younger students about Queen Elizabeth and the Elizabethan Age.

Rembrandt—Men of Genius series by Ellen M. Dolan

Though this is written for children to understand, it gives a wonderful understanding of the life and work of this Dutch painter, one of the most important artists in world history.

A Piece of the Mountain: The Story of Blaise Pascal by Joyce McPherson

A very well written, interesting story about the French mathematician and Christian apologist of the 1600s. Pascal is the man who gave us "Pascal's Wager" and spoke of the God-shaped vacuum in people. I really enjoy this book.

Fascinating Folks & Exciting Events

Galileo & The Scientific Revolution (1564–1642)

More than three hundred years before Jesus was born, a Greek named Aristotle developed several ideas about science (the earth, motion, human bodies, etc.). These ideas were accepted as fact for eighteen hundred years! During the 1500s, a few people began to question these ideas. One of the most important questioners was Galileo. In 1598, while he was a professor at the University of Pisa in Italy, Galileo challenged one of Aristotle's ideas—and he used an experiment to prove his challenge. Aristotle had taught that heavier objects would fall faster to the earth than lighter objects. It just made sense. However, Galileo discovered that it did not work that way.

The oft-told story is that he took a group of students to the Leaning Tower of Pisa and left them on the ground, along with other curious bystanders, to watch the results. Then Galileo climbed all the way to the top of the tower and, with great drama, released two cannonballs at the same time. One of the cannonballs weighed ten pounds and one of them weighed only one pound. If Aristotle's theory were right, the ten-pound ball would hit the ground first. If Galileo's theory were right, the balls would hit the ground together. Everyone watching must have held their breath as the young challenger took on the great Aristotle. And suddenly, eighteen hundred years of accepted belief crashed to the earth! Galileo was proven right when both cannonballs hit the earth together. This discovery is called the law of accelerating bodies. And, with the fall of Aristotle's theory, the Scientific Revolution began.

The Spanish Armada (1588)

Sometimes family squabbles get out of hand. The first daughter of King Henry VIII of England, Queen Mary, married a Spanish prince, Philip II, who soon became the King of Spain while she was Queen of England. The royal couple were committed Catholics, while England had become Protestant under Henry VIII. Mary died without any heirs after ruling England for only five years. The English people welcomed Queen Elizabeth (King Henry VIII's second daughter and Mary's half sister) as their new ruler for she was Protestant. King Philip II of Spain asked Elizabeth to marry him, but she promptly turned him down. Actually, lots of kings and princes asked Elizabeth to marry them, and she turned them all down. However, King Philip II was not happy about the loss of England, especially to a Protestant sister-in-law! To add fuel to the fire, Queen Elizabeth began supporting the Protestant Dutch revolt against Catholic Spain (ruled by you-know-who!). This made King Philip II very angry, which set the stage for big trouble. The straw that broke the camel's back was when Queen Elizabeth allowed her English "seadogs" to sail the Atlantic in order to capture Spanish galleons loaded down with New World gold. Sir Francis Drake, the first Englishman to sail all the way around the world, once brought Queen Elizabeth pirated Spanish gold that amounted to double England's national yearly income! King Philip II had had enough. He planned a huge invasion of England with his fleet of ships called the Spanish Armada.

But everything went wrong. First, Sir Francis Drake sailed into the main Spanish port and sunk lots of ships, delaying the sailing of the Armada for a whole year. Then, just before the Armada was to sail, the Spanish admiral died. When the Spanish fleet got to England, they were astonished by the quickness of the English ships, so they were reluctant to attack. After nine days of this, the Armada anchored off the coast of France, which was a big mistake. The English sent eight flaming ships ("fire ships") into the fleet. Many Spanish ships caught fire, others fled out into the Atlantic, where a terrible gale hit the Armada and swept them into the fierce North Sea. By the time it was done, half of the massive Spanish Armada had been sunk, and the English were entirely victorious. The glory and power of Spain, which had started in 1492 with Columbus, faded away in 1588 with the defeat of the Spanish Armada. And Philip really didn't like his sister-in-law!

Crossword Puzzle

Using the clues below and the words from your vocabulary list, fill in the crossword puzzle.

Cromwell
Drake
edict
England
expedition
France
Galileo
gravity
haven
Henry IV
Holland
independence
Newton
Peter the Great
Pietist
Puritan
revolt
separate
Spanish Armada
telescope

Across:

1 Queen Elizabeth's country.

4 The country that became a refuge for English protestants.

7 To divide.

9 The French protestants, Irish, and Dutch were all in _____ against the ruling government.

11 Also a Bible scholar, this man discovered the law of gravity.

13 Freedom from the control of others.

15 This French king converted to Catholicism to rule his country better.

16 This English sea captain was a favorite of Queen Elizabeth.

17 The _____ of Nantes gave the French Protestants rights they had never had before.

19 Francis Drake went on an _____ to the Spanish Main.

Down:

2 This scientist used the telescope to learn cool astronomy facts.

3 Isaac Newton discovered this when an apple hit him on his head.

4 A safe place.

5 The builder of St. Petersburg.

6 The Puritan who wouldn't be king.

8 A group in England who believed that the Church of England should be purified.

10 King Philip of Spain sent this against Queen Elizabeth of England.

12. An instrument for making distant objects appear nearer and larger.

14 A group in Germany who believed everyone needs a personal relationship with Jesus Christ.

18 Henry of Navarre (who became Henry IV), was king of this country.

Hands-On History Fun
Create-A-Craft:

Sparkly Suns

Louis XIV reigned as the King of France for forty-two years. During this time, he became known as the "Sun King" since everything in France revolved around him. Louis XIV believed that God had given him the right and responsibility to rule his country completely, so he put himself in charge of everything. When people talk about Louis XIV, they talk about an absolute monarchy, because he was in absolute control of absolutely everything. EVERYTHING!

You will need: ¼ cup salt; ¼ cup water; 1 plastic zipper bag; white poster board or construction paper; ¼ cup flour; 2 tablespoons yellow tempera paint; 1 paintbrush

In the zipper bag, place the salt, flour, water, and paint. Carefully remove as much air from the bag as possible, then seal the bag tightly. Gently knead the ingredients in the bag until thoroughly mixed. The mixture will be a textured paint. You may find it easier to paint if you pour this mixture into a small plastic bowl or styrofoam cup, but you may choose to paint straight from the bag. Now, with the paintbrush, paint fourteen suns on the poster board. When it is dry, you will have sparkly suns to remind you of Louis XIV, the Sun King.

Science Stuff:

Try Galileo's Experiment!

You will need: A large stuffed animal; A small stuffed animal; A large hardbound book with a rubber band around it; A small hardbound book with a rubber band around it; A small sized rock placed in a sock; A large sized rock placed in a sock; Or any other pairs of big and small stuff!

CAUTION: ADULT SUPERVISION REQUIRED. The "dropper" should stand on a chair or ladder to be up as high as possible. Have everyone else stand back but close enough to be able to see the results. The "dropper" should drop the stuffed animals at the same time from the same height. Did they hit the ground at the same time? Next, drop the hardbound books. Did they hit the ground at the same time? Finally, drop the socks. Did they hit the ground at the same time? What do you think? Was Galileo right, or was Aristotle right?

Where in the World . . .
is Spain?

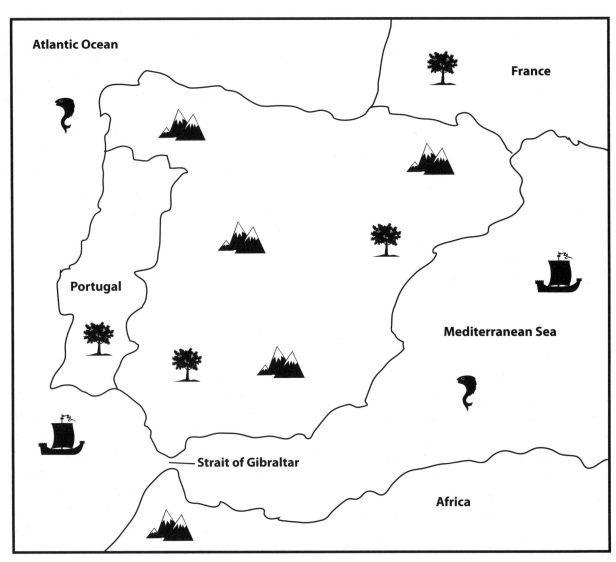

Color the areas around these:

blue water   purple mountains   green vegetation

Clues for finding Spain:

- I am EAST of the Atlantic Ocean.
- I am WEST of the Mediterranean Sea.
- I am NORTH of the Strait of Gibraltar.
- I am EAST of Portugal.

Where am I?

Your Own Masterpiece

Draw a picture of Sir Francis Drake attacking the Spanish ships.

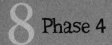

Creative Fun with History!
Going-Goofy Game:

Puritans, Separatists, and the Church of England

Players:

Puritan's team: Each player on this team needs to have a white cloth tied on his or her arm to symbolize that the Puritans wanted to purify the Church of England.

Separatist's team: Each player on this team needs to have a blue cloth tied on his or her arm to symbolize that the Separatists wanted to separate from the Church of England. That is why they left England and crossed the waters to go to Holland and then to America (these were the Pilgrims!).

Church of England: One person per turn to be "it."

You need to have an agreed-upon spot to be "jail."

This is basically a game of tag. The person designated to be the Church of England tries to tag each person in the game, regardless of his or her team membership. When a person is tagged, he or she goes immediately to "jail." When all the members of one team have been tagged, they lose, and the play ceases. A new Church of England player is chosen from the losing team, the teams trade cloths (becoming the opposite team in the process), and play resumes. Continue until exhausted!

To liven the game up a bit, you may choose to add this variation: When the Church of England approaches to tag you, you may hold your nose with one hand and your toe with the other, which will make you "safe." If you aren't able to hold that position, the Church of England can jail you.

Revivals & Revolutions

John Wesley

George Whitefield

Bible Verses to Read & Talk About

Which way? Proverbs 14:12, Psalm 37:5

This period of history was a time of great upheaval in Europe. In France, the people decided to get rid of their king and nobility and govern themselves. However, they wanted to find their source of laws in "man's reason" rather than God's truth. Read these Scriptures together and talk about what you learn.

- According to Proverbs, what happens when we follow our own ideas instead of God's? According to Psalm 37, what do you suppose happens when we follow God's plans instead?

Who is invited? Luke 14:15–24

In England and America there was a tremendous move of God known as The Great Awakening. George Whitefield and John Wesley, two of the best-known figures from The Great Awakening, preached to people who were not part of the church—many who were poor, dirty, and rough-mannered. Read this Scripture together and talk about whether Wesley and Whitefield were doing what Jesus described.

- Whom did Jesus describe as being invited first to the banquet? What did the people invited say? Who was invited next? How does this apply to people in the Church? Outside of the Church?

Suggested Books for Reading Together

The Runaway's Revenge: John Newton by Dave & Neta Jackson

Have you ever sung the hymn, "Amazing Grace"? It was written by an ex-slave trader named John Newton, and this is his story, told for children. One of the Trailblazer series.

The Chimney Sweep's Ransom: John Wesley by Dave & Neta Jackson

Another Trailblazer title, this story concerns a boy in the 1700s who works in the mines of England and is helped by John Wesley. It is worth the read.

John Wesley by May McNeer & Lynd Ward

This is a delightful book for children about the great preacher of the Methodist church (though he remained in the Anglican church his entire life!).

Captain Cook, Pacific Explorer by Ronald Syme

An excellent book for elementary children, showing the routes of Captain Cook's voyages in addition to the marvelous story of his life.

The Marquis de Lafayette, Bright Sword for Freedom—A World Landmark Book by Hodding Carter

Lafayette was a major figure just prior to the French Revolution. Unfortunately, when the Revolution began, it did not follow the Constitutional lines as did America. Instead, it exploded out of control. Read the fascinating story of what happened to Lafayette during this time. Great read-aloud.

Fascinating Folks & Exciting Events

The Great Awakening (1730s–1790s)

At the beginning of the eighteenth century, England and America were places where Christianity was considered a set of rules and regulations. It was a place where the few people who went to church did so mostly out of an attitude of "this is what we have always done." There was also drunkenness, immorality, restlessness, and brutality throughout the land. It seemed hopeless. But then, God began to move in mighty ways: in 1734, a preacher named Jonathan Edwards suddenly saw amazing responses to the Word of God. Nearly his whole small New England town began to come to church, and people became serious about God and living in obedience to Him.

This move of God began to sweep the New England area with powerful results. Over in England, in 1738, an Anglican minister named John Wesley found wonderful assurance that God had forgiven him of his sins. He began to preach across England telling people that they needed to know God, not just know about Him. One of his good friends, George Whitefield, also came to know the boundless mercy and grace of God. He became one of the most powerful preachers in church history. It is said that he could be heard by 30,000 people at a time—without the use of microphones!

Both John Wesley (in England) and George Whitefield (in America and England) preached outdoors since the State churches usually closed their doors to them. They preached to poor people who had never before heard the gospel; they preached to government officials; they preached to rich and powerful people, and to people others had given up on. And God blessed their preaching! People were changed; villages and towns were changed; regions were changed; and the history of nations was changed. Historians often credit the Great Awakening with saving England from the violent revolution that nearly destroyed France. Many American scholars say that it was the Great Awakening that put such immense strength into the souls of Americans that they would be able to fight against impossible odds and win the American Revolution. The Great Awakening! We need to be thankful for what God has done in the past and prayerful that He will do it again!

Word Scrambles

Unscramble the words to spell out people, places, or things that have to do with this time period. Look at the vocabulary list at the bottom for possible answers and don't get too "mixed up!"

atgre wakeangni _____

tionurevol _____

valrevi _____

incapat koco _____

eldfiwheti _____

edwsrad _____

leywes _____

tnyrany _____

quaeliyt _____

xle rxe _____

ghtenlientenm _____

bertliy _____

odistmeth _____

tienarint _____

iontdecrala _____

tervcon _____

edunit atests _____

iescolno _____

alssur _____

lamor _____

gutineillo _____

Captain Cook	colonies	convert	declaration	Edwards
Enlightenment	equality	Great Awakening	guillotine	itinerant
Lex Rex	liberty	Methodist	moral	revival
revolution	Russia	tyranny	United States	Whitefield
Wesley				

Hands-On History Fun
Create-A-Craft:

Make Your Own Quill Pen

When the signers of the Declaration of Independence in America signed their names in 1776, they used a quill pen made from a bird feather.

You will need: A bird feather (turkey is great)—available at craft stores, or your local turkey; Scissors or a sharp knife; Tempera Paint, thinned with a little water; Paper on which to write your "John Hancock" (that means, your name)

CAUTION: ADULT SUPERVISION REQUIRED. Holding the feather carefully, cut the end off at a slant to give a nice point. You will need to cover the end of your pen with ink by dipping the cut part of the feather into the thinned tempera paint. Now, try writing your name on the paper. It may take some practice!

Fun Food to Fix:

Captain Cook's Sea Biscuits

When Captain Cook, his passengers, and the crew sailed to the South Pacific, they needed food that would keep a LONG time! Try this version of "hard tack" and see what you think.

You will need: 1½ cups flour; 1 teaspoon salt; ½ cup water

Mix the flour and salt together in a large bowl. Add water, a few drops at a time, and mix until you have a stiff dough. Rollout the dough on a board sprinkled with flour to a thickness of about one-third of an inch. Cut the dough into squares. Use a fork to prick the top of the biscuits. Now, bake them at 375 degrees for about 25 minutes, or until they turn lightly brown. To store, place them in a tightly covered container.

Where in the World . . .

is Australia?

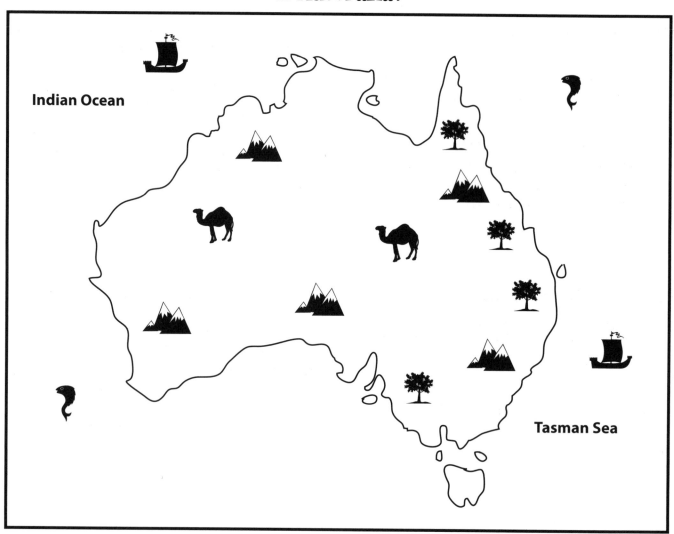

Color the areas around these:

 **blue water**

 purple mountains

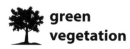 **green vegetation**

 **yellow desert**

Clues for finding Australia:

- I am an ISLAND.
- I am SOUTH and EAST of the Indian Ocean.
- I am WEST of the Tasman Sea.

Where am I?

As a fun activity, find Australia on a world map and see how big it is compared to. . . the United States . . . China . . . New Zealand . . . Europe . . . Greenland . . . the state, province, or country you live in!

Your Own Masterpiece

Draw a picture depicting Captain Cook's landing on New Zealand's shore.

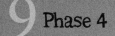

Creative Fun with History!
Singing Somewhat Silly Songs:

Count von Zinzendorf & the Moravians (To the tune of "Row, Row, Row Your Boat")

Count von Zin-zen-dorf,
Have you any news?
Do the people get along?
Which path will they choose?

From so many parts
Yonder did they come.
Noisy and differing! They're all a-squabb-a-ling!
It's quite troublesome!

This, that, the other too,
Morning, noon and night.
Bick-er-ing, chal-leng-ing, ar-gu-ing, quib-bil-ing
Goodness, what a sight!

Count von Zin-zen-dorf,
Tell me what you'll do!
What on earth can help these folks?
What can make things new?

"Pray, pray, fast and pray,
Pray, and pray some more.
Hum-ble our-selves in the sight of the Lord
And for His grace implore!"

Oh, my, what is this?
What news do you bring?
Something so great is now happening here,
A truly glad-some thing!

God moved by His grace.
People changed that day!
Zin-zen-dorf and the Mor-a-vi-ans found
Peace through Christ, the Way!

So, they got along
Famously, it seems.
Wor-ship-ing, for-giv-ing, much-pray-ing, min-ist-'ring,
Wow! It's not a dream!